RADIO TI

JOURNAL OF THE BRITISH BROADCASTII

The War Years

Classic covers, articles and
illustrations from the archive
1939–1946

Contents

I GO FURTHER WITH COCOA

RadioTimes

EDITORS
Shem Law, Tom Loxley

DESIGN & ART DIRECTION
Jacob Howard

COPY EDITORS
Patrick Mulkern, Ron Hewit

PICTURE RESEARCH
Rachel Young

MANAGING EDITOR
Claire Hollingsworth

HEAD OF HERITAGE
Ralph Montagu

**PRODUCTION &
AD SERVICES DIRECTOR**
Sharon Thompson

PRODUCTION MANAGER
Steve Calver

PUBLISHER
Ben Head

PUBLISHING DIRECTOR
Zoe Helme

MANAGING DIRECTOR
Dominic Murray

REPRO by Rhapsody

PRINTED by Ancient House Press

IMAGES SUPPLIED BY
Radio Times Archive, Getty,
Museum of London, BBC Photosales

Radio Times would like to thank
all staff members, freelance
contributors, writers and
illustrators – past and present

Published by Immediate Media Company
London Ltd, Vineyard House, 44 Brook Green,
London W6 7BT. Published in the United
Kingdom 2021. *Radio Times* is part of
Immediate Media Company London Ltd.

ISBN 978-0-9929364-7-1

RT goes to war

When the Second World War began in September 1939, it was up to BBC Radio – and *Radio Times* – to keep the British public informed and entertained

FOREWORD BY **SHEM LAW** CO-EDITOR *RADIO TIMES*

WELCOME TO THE latest project from *Radio Times*. *The War Years* is a project very close to our hearts and, we hope, to yours. Every year, there are many TV and radio programmes broadcast about the Second World War, the majority of which mark anniversaries of campaigns or battles on land, on sea and in the air.

However, the war on the home front was a seemingly never-ending six-year slog for the citizens of Great Britain, a period that involved increasing privations and sacrifice.

The BBC and *Radio Times* were beacons of hope during that time. The wireless was, for most, the only source of up-to-the-minute

> **❝ The BBC and *Radio Times* were beacons of hope during that time ❞**

news about the war and provided a much-needed escape from the realities of rationing, queues and nights spent in air-raid shelters.

Looking through the issues of *Radio Times* from September 1939 until the end of the war in 1945 and into 1946, you can see that the BBC commissioned more radio comedy than ever before.

Comedians and popular musical and variety acts played throughout the day on shows such as *Workers' Playtime* and *Music while You Work*. News was important, but the morale of the nation was even more crucial.

The BBC also became an integral part of the war effort – from providing listening services, which would monitor foreign and enemy broadcasts, to expanding its overseas broadcasting into many occupied countries.

The listings in *Radio Times* are the only day-to-day record of what was broadcast each day. Reading this source material now gives a fascinating insight into a nation at war – and it was of course written when no one knew how the war would play out. The words and tone can feel old-fashioned more than seven decades on, but they are also at times profoundly moving.

Along with the articles and listings, some of the most interesting and valuable material from a social-history point of view are the advertisements that appeared in the magazine. Some were for companies and brands that still exist today, informing the reader how they were helping the war effort, and there were also important announcements from the Ministry of Information on rationing or recruitment drives. They build an engrossing picture of what were the paramount themes of the day.

As the war progressed, paper rationing meant that issues became smaller and smaller, with only the most vital comment finding space in the two-page "features section", and in the latter years of the war colour inks were banned, even for the Christmas issues.

It was a time of grinding austerity and truly heroic stoicism. But never once in the 300 or so issues that we've gone through did we find any hint of defeatism, self-pity or wanton propaganda. Perhaps that's something that media outlets today could learn from in a time of national crisis.

Reading the original articles that appear in these pages, you gain an insight into the programmes of the time. At least one survives – read about the first *Desert Island Discs* on page 72. And you can also still hear occasional episodes of *ITMA (It's That Man Again)* on Radio 4 Extra – you can meet the characters who inhabited the *ITMA* world on page 32. It's interesting to see how two great national institutions began life.

It's a great honour to present to you the work of *Radio Times* colleagues past and present. It shows clearly that my job of co-editing this great magazine is less a case of bringing you the best of TV and radio, and more of being a custodian of a nationally important record of social history. 🐾

PROGRAMMES FOR
June 23—29

TIMES
H BROADCASTING CORPORATION

(ATING WORLD-RADIO)

A. RETAILER

now WEBBING EQUIPMENT

now MESS-TINS

now PARACHUTES

now HEADPHONES

now FOR FLYING HELMETS

now HAND GRENADES

now GAS MASKS

now FOR ANTI-GAS OINTMENTS

now AMMUNITION CARRIERS

y 11, 1941 Vol. 72 No. 928   Registered at the G.P.O. as a Newspaper

PROGRAMMES FOR
July 13—19

WOPENCE

ADIO TIMES
NAL OF THE BRITISH BROADCASTING CORPORATION

(INCORPORATING WORLD-RADIO)

S THAT
ND AGAIN!'

s is Tommy Handley enjoying
can Funf be far behind?). You
joy it too by listening to them
S.A.' on Friday evenings.

dway Calling—
ain replies all-star ENSA exchange (p. 8)

idsummer Night's Dream'
enes from Shakespeare's play (p. 9)

Fourteenth of July'
moration of France's National Day (p. 13)

menade Concerts
broadcasts this week (pp. 13, 21, 29)

Human Bondage'
play, 'Mildred Rogers', adapted from
Somerset Maugham's novel (p. 16)

de Striking Force'

THURSDAY Home Service

203.5 m. 14

BLACK-OUT STARTS—	
London 5.25	Plymouth 5.48
Cardiff 5.37	Leeds 5.19
Edinburgh 5.12	Aberdeen 4.59

A.M.

7.1

7.1
Reco
trali

7.30
' Mac   (Children's Hour Director)

Christmas

10.30 a.m.
CHRISTMAS MORNING
with an address by the Dean

2.0 p.m.
'TO ABSENT FR
etings to the men and women
fighting in the cause of f

3.30 (Forces)

TURN THAT LIGHT OUT!
For many nights during the war, homes,
businesses and streets were blacked
out. Every day *Radio Times* provided the
required start times up and down the UK.

LEFT covers from June 1940 and July 1941
reflecting a diet of combat and mirth.

RADIO ✳ TIMES
JOURNAL OF THE BRITISH BROADCASTING CORPORATION
The war years 1939

1939

"THIS COUNTRY IS AT WAR WITH GERMANY"

A newspaper seller on the Strand in London on 3 September 1939 carrying confirmation of the news delivered to the nation on BBC Radio the same morning by the prime minister, Neville Chamberlain (below).

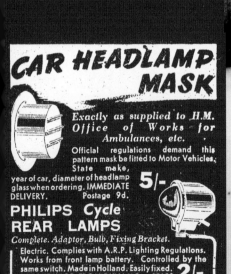

Before the storm

In the weeks leading up to the declaration of war, *Radio Times* produced its usual fun and colourful front covers. However, that would soon change... 🐿

RADIO TIMES
JOURNAL OF THE BRITISH BROADCASTING CORPORATION

The war years 1939

THE FIRST WEEK

Ready for anything

The threat of war with Germany had been in the air for months, so it was no surprise that when the declaration of war finally came, the BBC's plans to continue broadcasting during the conflict were already in place...

RADIO TIMES **SUPPLEMENTARY** ISSUE, September 4, 1939, Vol. 64, No. 831A

Registered at the G.P.O. as a Newspaper

Price TWOPENCE

RADIO TIMES

JOURNAL OF THE BRITISH BROADCASTING CORPORATION

(INCORPORATING WORLD-RADIO)

REVISED PROGRAMMES for Sept. 4-10

OADCASTING CARRIES O

Radio Times, September 1, 1939. Vol. 64 No. 831
Registered at the G.P.O. as a Newspaper

Price TWOPENCE

RADIO TIMES

JOURNAL OF THE BRITISH BROADCASTING CORPORATION

PROGRAMMES FOR SEPTEMBER 3–9

J. B. Priestley

will read the first instalment of his new serial novel

'LET THE PEOPLE SING'

on Sunday

ALSO THIS WEEK

'The Four Feathers'
First instalment of a serial version of
A. E. W. Mason's story

'Rescue'
Story of the lifeboat service

The St. Leger
Commentary from Doncaster

'Further Outlook Warmer'
Farcical comedy

'Wireless Puppets'
with Davy Burnaby and Phyllis Monkman

Militia Camp
Sing Song

SWINGING INTO ACTION

When war was declared on 3 September 1939, the issue of *Radio Times* for the week 3–9 September with JB Priestley on the cover (left) was already in circulation. The news of the coming war meant that the BBC had to revise its schedules and issue a supplementary edition of *Radio Times* (pictured above), but the Corporation was not caught entirely unprepared.

The editorial (opposite) made it clear that the BBC had been planning for the outbreak of war for almost a year and, in a practical and upbeat tone, it laid out plans to serve up a daily schedule of radio programmes from 7.00am to midnight comprising plays, music, talks, features, religious services and comedy – with news on the hour, every hour. The BBC Television service had been suspended completely on 1 September.

It was just as well *Radio Times* was prepared, too – this was the second of three issues that staff had to produce in just one week. The editorial also stressed that *Radio Times* would soldier on, albeit in reduced form whenever paper supplies were short, stating simply that, "We shall do our best to bring you the full and correct information about all the doings and plans of the BBC."

RADIO TIMES
JOURNAL OF THE BRITISH BROADCASTING CORPORATION
The war years 1939

RADIO TIMES

Broadcasting Carries On !

Broadcasting carries on !

That is the slogan of the BBC in this hour of national endeavour, when the British nation is nerving itself for the greatest effort it has ever made. In every department of life the British people are steeling themselves for their great task. Broadcasting intends to help in the work, whatever the difficulties may be.

* * * *

For nearly a year now the BBC has been making its plans. Recognising the part that broadcasting would play in the struggle, it could not afford to leave anything to chance.

First of all, of course, radio will be one of the chief means of communication during the war. That has already been proved. The Government can speak to the people—news can reach the remotest village—instructions can be issued by the Ministries —warnings can be given of approaching attacks.

* * * *

These are obvious functions of radio during a war, and their vital importance is recognised by everyone. But there is another function that is nearly as important, and that is entertainment. Broadcasting can help to take our minds off the horrors of war as nothing else can.

That is why the BBC has not been content to plan programmes consisting merely of gramophone records alternating with news. Even in the dislocation of the first few days, some of your favourite talkers have been coming to the microphone, the BBC Theatre Organist has been at his post to entertain you, and the hope and comfort of religious services have not been withheld from the listener, at whatever cost to those taking part. But from next Wednesday, if all goes well, all-day 'live' programmes will begin. Broadcasting will still run from seven o'clock in the morning till after midnight (with news broadcasts in the intervening hours whenever there is any important news), but the programmes broadcast will be real, presented entertainment, studded with plays, musical comedies, features, talks ; in fact ordinary broadcast programmes—only probably of a rather higher standard than those we know in times of peace ! There will even be a Children's Hour, and regular broadcasts to schools.

* * * *

We said ' if all goes well '. Every listener will realise that there will be times when these programmes cannot be carried out. There are endless possibilities of hitches, no matter how carefully plans may have been laid in advance. If the announcer has to say that a programme that has been published in the RADIO TIMES cannot be broadcast, listeners will understand.

On the other hand, there may easily be occasions when programmes are changed only to be improved. In these early stages, when so many things have still to be learnt from experience, it may be found when the time comes that a better programme than the one published can be given. Listeners will understand if that happens, too.

* * * *

Writing as we are doing at the very moment of decision, it is hard to foresee what conditions will be, even by the time this extra number of the RADIO TIMES appears. But the difficulties of keeping broadcasting going in time of war can hardly be over-estimated. Many a broadcaster may have to risk his life to supply you with your entertainment and your news. But broadcasting is going on.

* * * *

London, the most obviously vulnerable centre in the British Isles, has ceased to be the centre of British broadcasting. Far away in other parts of the country, in new premises specially reserved for this time of need, are the centres from which your programmes come. At one centre is a team of Variety

RADIO ⚜ TIMES
JOURNAL OF THE BRITISH BROADCASTING CORPORATION

The war years 1939
RADIO TIMES SUPPLEMENTARY ISSUE DATED SEPTEMBER 4, 1939

FIRST STEPS in FIRST AID

You should keep this page handy for reference during the broadcasts. These diagrams will be referred to in the talks.

An easy course for everyone will be given in five talks by a doctor on Monday, Tuesday, Wednesday, Thursday, and Friday this week at 6.25 p.m.

Full courses for those seeking a diploma in First Aid are given by the following organisations:

British Red Cross Society,
14, Grosvenor Crescent, London, S.W.1.

St. John Ambulance Association,
St. John's Gate, London, E.C.1.

British Red Cross Society (Scottish Branch),
206, Bath Street, Glasgow, C.2.

St. Andrew's Ambulance Association,
108, North Street, Glasgow.

Full information about how to learn will be given in the broadcast talks.

Triangular bandage applied to the foot. It is made to ensheath the foot and ankle. The ends are brought round the leg above the ankle, and the apex of the bandage is pulled upwards. The ends are tied in front. The apex, shown pointing up the leg, is then brought downwards and pinned over the top of the foot.

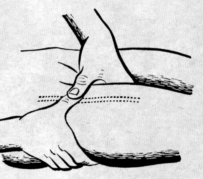

Pressure applied by both thumbs to the pressure point of the right femoral artery in the groin. This is used in cases of severe bleeding from the lower part of the thigh or leg.

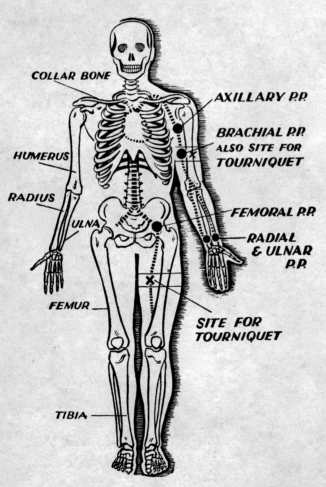

COLLAR BONE

AXILLARY P.P.

BRACHIAL P.P.
ALSO SITE FOR
TOURNIQUET

HUMERUS

RADIUS

ULNA

FEMORAL P.P.

RADIAL
& ULNAR
P.P.

FEMUR

SITE FOR
TOURNIQUET

TIBIA

Diagram showing bones and main arteries of the body. The discs indicate pressure points. Each of these is on the course of a main artery. Pressure at one of these points will stop most of the blood passing into the limb beyond.

Compound fracture of the leg. The shin bone is protruding through the skin.

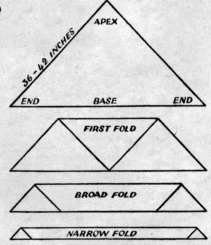

36 - 42 INCHES · APEX

END · BASE · END

FIRST FOLD

BROAD FOLD

NARROW FOLD

The triangular bandage is of prime importance in first-aid work. It can be made from calico or linen. A large scarf or handkerchief can be used. It should measure 36-42 inches from the apex to either end. Large and small slings are readily made. As a bandage it is used in the form of a 'broad-fold' or 'narrow-fold'. To make a broad-fold, fold the apex to the base, then fold the upper edge to the base again. To make a narrow-fold, fold it once again.

FIRST STEPS in FIRST AID

This evening at 6.25 a well-known London doctor will give the first of a series of practical talks on things you should know about First Aid. He speaks again on Tuesday, Wednesday, Thursday, Friday and Saturday

(See diagrams on page 5)

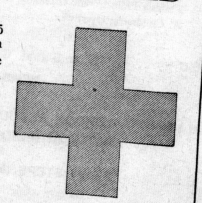

'It's rather hard to tell you who is winning,
as all the horses are camouflaged'

SUPPLEMENTARY ISSUE DATED SEPTEMBER 4, 1939

STOP PRESS

late programme alterations will be inserted on this page

CROSSWORD 339: Solution

A SERIOUS BUSINESS

RT's pages carried tips on first aid, information on programme changes and a plug for its sister publication *The Listener*. But there was also room for humour, too, with cartoons (top right).

The war years 1939

Radio Times. September 8, 1939. Vol. 64 No. 832
Registered at the G.P.O. as a Newspaper

Price TWOPENCE

RADIO ✴ TIMES
JOURNAL OF THE BRITISH BROADCASTING CORPORATION
(INCORPORATING WORLD-RADIO)

Detailed BBC Programmes for September 10—16

Keep the home fires burning

Anti-clockwise from left: in the early weeks of the war the magazine's covers reflected patriotism, practicality and a sense of national unity — Big Ben and the clock tower at the Palace of Westminster; a row of idyllic country cottages at Snowhill in Gloucestershire with the cover line that reads "There'll always be an England!"; and a group of cheerful miners "somewhere in Wales" who were digging for victory.

Inside, the listings offered up classical music and broadcasts such as *Bee-keeping: Preparations for Winter* and light entertainment programmes starring the likes of Gracie Fields and Arthur Askey. There were also reminders (opposite) that listeners could tune in to foreign broadcasts from all over the world on short wave, from Ankara to the Vatican and all points in between.

Radio Times. September 15, 1939. Vol. 64 No. 833
Registered at the G.P.O. as a Newspaper

Price TWOPENCE

RADIO ✴ TIMES
JOURNAL OF THE BRITISH BROADCASTING CORPORATION
(INCORPORATING WORLD-RADIO)

Detailed BBC Programmes for September 17—23

'There'll always be an England!'

Radio Times. October 13, 1939. Vol. 65 No. 837 Registered at the G.P.O. as a Newspaper

PRICE TWOPENCE

PROGRAMMES FOR
October 15—21

RADIO ✴ TIMES
JOURNAL OF THE BRITISH BROADCASTING CORPORATION
(INCORPORATING WORLD-RADIO)

KEEPING THE HOME FIRES BURNING

In war as in peace, the work of miners, like those pictured here 'somewhere in Wales', remains of first importance to the well-being of the nation. A 'Home Front' programme on Wednesday will present a radio picture of the reaction in pits and homes to the new conditions.

14

FOREIGN STATIONS YOU CAN HEAR

These are the normal wavelengths. Any wartime changes will be made as they are known.

LONG AND MEDIUM WAVE

kc/s	m.	kW	Station
			Band No. 1. 150–300 kc/s.
160	1875	120	Hilversum (No. 1) (Holland) (10 kW only until 7.40 p.m.)
172	1744	500	Moscow (No. 1) (U.S.S.R.)
182	1648	80	Radio-Paris (France)
216	1389	150	Motala (Sweden)
232	1293	150	Luxembourg
240	1250	60	Kalundborg (Denmark)
271	1107	100	Leningrad (No. 1) (U.S.S.R.)
			Band No. 3. 500–1,500 kc/s.
546	549.5	120	Budapest (No. 1) (Hungary)
556	539.6	100	Beromünster (Switzerland)
565	531	100	Radio-Eireann (Eire)
601	499.2	20	Rabat (Morocco)
610	491.8	20	Florence (No. 1) (Italy)
620	483.9	15	Brussels (No. 1) (Belgium)

kc/s	m.	kW	Station
648	463	100	Lyons (PTT) (France)
677	443.1	100	Sottens (Switzerland)
686	437.3	20	Belgrade (Yugoslavia)
695	431.7	120	Paris (PTT) (France)
704	426.1	55	Stockholm (Sweden)
713	420.8	100	Rome (No. 1) (Italy)
724	414.4	17	Hilversum (Jaarsveld) (Holland). Relays Hilversum (No. 1)
749	400.5	100	Marseilles (PTT) (France)
776	386.6	120	Toulouse (PTT) (France)
814	368.6	50	Milan (No. 1) (Italy)
859	349.2	100	Strasbourg (France)
913	328.6	70	Toulouse (Radio - Toulouse) (France)
932	321.9	15	Brussels (No. 2) (Belgium)
959	312.8	60	Poste Parisien (France)
995	301.5	65	Hilversum (No. 2) (Holland) (15 kW only until 7.40 p.m.)

kc/s	m.	kW	Station
1040	288.5	120	Rennes-Bretagne (France)
1059	283.3	20	Bari (No. 1) (Italy)
1077	278.6	60	Bordeaux-Lafayette (France)
1095	274	20	Radio-Normandie (France)
1131	265.3	60	Hörby (Sweden)
1140	263.2	30	Turin (No. 1) (Italy)
1167	257.1	15	Monte Ceneri (Switzerland)
1185	253.2	60	Nice-Côte d'Azur (France)
1213	247.3	60	Lille (Radio PTT Nord) (France)
1222	245.5	60	Rome (No. 2) (Italy)
1258	238.5	15	Riga (Latvia)
		20	Radio-Nacional (Spain)
1303	230.2	10	Naples (No. 1) (Italy)
1312	228.7	2.5	Malmö (Sweden)
1321	227.1	27	Radio-Méditerranée (France)
1366	219.6	35	Bordeaux-Sud-Ouest (France)
1393	215.4	25	Radio-Lyons (France)
1420	211.3	10	Vaasa (Finland)
1456	206	5	Eiffel Tower (Paris) (France)

SHORT WAVE

Mc/s	m.	kW	Call	Station and Time Schedule
6.00	50	20	RNE	Moscow (U.S.S.R.).
6.03	49.75	100	RW96	Moscow (U.S.S.R.).
6.03	49.75	25	HVJ	Vatican City.
6.06	49.5	10	WCAI	Philadelphia (Pa., U.S.A.).
6.06	49.46	12	SBO	Motala (Sweden). 21.15–22.00.
6.09	49.24	15	OAX4Z	Lima (Peru). 01.00–07.30.
6.10	49.18	25	WNBI	Bound Brook (N.J., U.S.A.).
6.10	49.18	1	YUA	Belgrade (Yugoslavia).
6.12	49.02	10	W2XE	Wayne (N.J., U.S.A.).
6.14	48.86	28	WPIT	Pittsburgh (Pa., U.S.A.).
6.15	48.78	2	CJRO	Winnipeg (Canada). 23.00–05.00.
6.17	48.62	10	W2XE	Wayne (N.J., U.S.A.).
6.19	48.47	25	HVJ	Vatican City.
6.35	47.21	50	IAC	Rome (Italy).
6.67	44.94	20	HBQ	Radio-Nations (Prangins, Switzerland).
7.03	42.7	..	EAQ1	Barcelona (Spain).
7.07	42.43	0.25	FETJ	Valladolid (Spain).
7.07	42.43	..	EA1BO	Burgos (Spain).
7.26	41.32	10	CSW8	Lisbon (Portugal).
7.28	41.21	25	TPB7	Paris (Radio-Mondial, France)
7.28	41.21	25	TPB11	Paris (Radio-Mondial, France)
7.36	40.76	15	RWG	Moscow (U.S.S.R.).
7.51	39.89	25	RKI	Moscow (U.S.S.R.).
8.83	33.99	5	COCQ	Havana (Cuba). 12.00–06.00.
9.12	32.88	5	HAT4	Budapest (Hungary).
9.34	32.1	20	HBL	Radio-Nations (Prangins, Switzerland).
9.46	31.7	20	TAP	Ankara (Turkey). 17.30–23.00.
9.50	31.58	1	OFD	Lahti (No. 2) (Finland). 18.15–23.00.
9.50	31.58	10	XEWW	Mexico City (Mexico).
9.50	31.58	12	PRF5	Rio de Janeiro (Brazil). W'days 22.45–23.00.
9.51	31.55	5	VK3ME	Melbourne (Australia). W'days 10.00–13.00.
9.52	31.51	100	RW96	Moscow (U.S.S.R.).
9.53	31.48	100	WGEO	Schenectady (N.Y., U.S.A.).
9.53	31.48	10	VUC2	Calcutta (India). 08.00–10.00.
9.53	31.46	12	SBU	Motala (Sweden). 22.15–23.00.
9.55	31.41	25	HVJ	Vatican City.
9.55	31.41	20-25	WGEA	Schenectady (N.Y., U.S.A.).
9.55	31.4	10	VUB2	Bombay (India).
9.56	31.37	10	OAX4T	Lima (Peru). 22.00–00.15.
9.57	31.35	10	WBOS	Millis (Boston) (Mass., U.S.A.). 14.00–06.00.
9.58	31.32	2	VLR	Melbourne (Australia).
9.59	31.28	20	VK2ME	Sydney (Australia). Sun. 06.00–08.00 ; 10.30–14.30 ; Mon. 16.30–18.30.
9.59	31.28	60	PCJ	Huizen (Holland) (Exp'tl.).
9.59	31.28	10	WCAI	Philadelphia (U.S.A.).
9.59	31.28	10	VUD2	Delhi (No. 2) (India).
9.60	31.25	20	RAL	Moscow (U.S.S.R.).
9.61	31.23	5	ZRL	Cape Town (S. Africa). 05.45–06.50 ; 09.30–13.00 ; 15.00–17.45.
9.61	31.22	5	LLG	Oslo (Norway). 20.00–07.00.
9.62	31.17	..	HAD	Budapest (Hungary) 00.00–03.00.
9.63	31.15	100	I2RO3	Rome (Italy).
9.63	31.13	25	I2RO3	Rome (Italy).
9.65	31.09	10	W2XE	Wayne (N.J., U.S.A.).
9.65	31.09	2	CS2WA	Lisbon. Tues., Thurs., Sat., 21.00–00.00.
9.66	31.06	25	HVJ	Vatican City.
9.66	31.06	7.5	LRX	Buenos Aires (Argentine). 15.15–04.00.
9.67	31.02	25	I2RO9	Rome (Italy).
9.68	30.98	10	TGWA	Guatemala City. 16.00–17.30 ; Sun. 16.30–06.00.
9.69	30.96	10	LRA1	Buenos Aires. Mon. to Thurs. 00.00–03.00 ; Fri. 22.00–03.00 ; Sat. and Sun. 01.00–03.00.

Mc/s	m.	kW	Call	Station and Time Schedule
9.74	30.8	10	CSW7	Lisbon (Portugal).
9.83	30.52	30	IRF	Rome (Italy).
9.86	30.43	20	EAQ	Madrid (Spain). 22.00–02.45.
10.22	29.35	15	PSH	Marapicú (Brazil). Mon. 02.00–02.30.
10.35	28.99	12	LSX	Buenos Aires (Argentine). Fri. 22.00–23.50.
11.04	27.17	10	CSW6	Lisbon (Portugal).
11.40	26.31	20	HBO	Radio-Nations (Prangins, Switzerland).
11.67	25.7	..	IGY	Rome (Italy).
11.70	25.63	12	SBP	Motala (Sweden). 19.00–22.15.
11.71	25.62	15	RIA	Moscow (U.S.S.R.).
11.72	25.6	12	TPA4	Paris (Radio-Mondial, France).
11.72	25.6	2	CJRX	Winnipeg (Canada). 23.00–09.00.
11.73	25.58	20	PHI	Huizen (Holland).
11.73	25.56	5	LKQ	Oslo (Norway). 00.00–04.00.
11.74	25.55	25	HVJ	Vatican City.
11.80	25.42	50	JZJ	Tokio (Japan).
11.81	25.4	100	I2RO4	Rome (Italy).
11.83	25.36	10	W2XE	Wayne (N.J., U.S.A.).
11.84	25.34	10	CSW5	Lisbon (Portugal).
11.85	25.31	.	HAD	Budapest (Hungary). 20.00–00.00.
11.87	25.28	10	VUM2	Madras (India). 09.30–10.00.
11.87	25.26	24	WPIT	Pittsburgh (Pa., U.S.A.).
11.88	25.25	2	VLR3	Melbourne (Australia).
11.88	25.24	12	TPA3	Paris (Radio-Mondial, France).
11.90	25.21	35	XGOY	Chungking (China). 11.30–17.30 ; 22.30–00.20.
12.00	25	20	RNE	Moscow (U.S.S.R.).
12.23	24.52	7.5	TFJ	Reykjavik (Iceland).
14.54	20.64	20	HBJ	Radio-Nations (Prangins, Switzerland).
14.79	20.28	..	IQA	Rome (Italy).
14.93	20.08	15	PSE	Marapicú (Brazil).
15.04	19.95	25	RKI	Moscow (U.S.S.R.).
15.12	19.84	25	HVJ	Vatican City.
15.13	19.83	25	TPB6	Paris (Radio-Mondial, France).
15.15	19.8	12	SBT	Motala (Sweden). 19.00–22.15.
15.16	19.79	50	JZK	Tokio (Japan).
15.17	19.78	5	LKV	Oslo (Norway). 16.00–00.00.
15.18	19.76	100	RW96	Moscow (U.S.S.R.).
15.20	19.74	20	TAQ	Ankara (Turkey). 11.30–13.00.
15.21	19.72	18	WPIT	Pittsburgh (Pa., U.S.A.).
15.21	19.72	10	CSW4	Lisbon (Portugal).
15.22	19.71	60	PCJ2	Huizen (Holland) (Exp'tl).
15.23	19.7	.	I2RO14	Rome (Italy).
15.24	19.68	12	TPA2	Paris (Radio-Mondial, France).
15.27	19.65	10	WCAI	Philadelphia (U.S.A.).
15.29	19.62	10	VUD4	Delhi (India).
15.30	19.61	50	I2RO6	Rome (Italy).
15.33	19.57	20-25	WGEA	Schenectady (N.Y., U.S.A.).
15.37	19.52	5	HAS3	Budapest (Hungary).
15.50	19.35	15	RAL	Moscow (U.S.S.R.).
17.75	16.9	5	LKW	Oslo (Norway).
17.77	16.88	20	PHI	Huizen (Holland).
17.78	16.87	25	WNBI	Bound Brook
17.78	16.87	50	JZL	Tokio (Japan).
17.82	16.84	50	I2RO8	Rome (Italy).
17.83	16.83	10	W2XE	Wayne (N.J.,
17.85	16.81	25	TPB3	Paris (Radio-
18.48	16.23	20	HBH	Radio-Nations
21.50	13.95	20-25	WGEA	Schenectady
21.52	13.94	10	WCAI	Philadelphia
21.54	13.93	6	WPIT	Pittsburgh (Pa

13

Radio Times (incorporating World-Radio), November 17, 1939

RADIO TIMES

2ᴰ

CLIXBY
WATSON

Woman's Number

BLUSHER & BALACLAVAS

Women were front and centre in this special Woman's Number from November with its illustration by Clixby Watson. Inside, there were tips for housewives on how to eke out food and clothing. But there was a broader message, too – "You will not inspire your family (nor help to win the war) by looking dowdy."

The evacuation of women and children from cities to the countryside had split families apart, so housewives were advised on how they could fill the lonely evenings. The central message: "It's a mistake to brood."

But it wasn't all about pulling yourself together and carrying on, or winning the war with a dab of lipstick. There were also hints of women beginning to take on more responsibility, with tales of secretaries setting up offices in school changing rooms, or training to become firefighters and air-raid wardens.

ELSIE AND DORIS WATERS. Radio's Gert and Daisy will broadcast three times this week—in Mid-Week Matinée, in the Children's Hour, and in Garrison Theatre.

SISTER ACT

Elsie and Doris Waters featured on the cover in December. Their comedy characters Gert and Daisy helped entertain the country right through the war years.

BALLOONS
or
Squaring the Circle!
By Bruce Sievier

We have received this amusing verse from the well-known broadcaster who is now Flying-Officer R. B. B. Sievier, M.C. (R.A.F.V.R.), of the Balloon Barrage

When I was but a baby boy
In coat and pantaloon,
My nurse would wheel me in the park
Behind a toy balloon.

When I arrived at walking stage
(An artful little mite!)
I used to buy a ball of string
And fly a baby kite.

But now I'm virile, big and strong,
I work from noon to noon
And all day long I sit beneath
A ruddy ' big ' balloon!

The moral of this story is
Enough to drive one wild,
For those who try to wage a war
Just treat one as a child!

Knit this Balaclava Helmet !

MATERIALS
3 oz. of 4-ply wool.
Two No. 10 needles and two No. 12 needles.

ABBREVIATIONS
K.—Knit ; P.—Purl ; St.—Stitch ; In.—Inches ; Tog.—Together ; Rep.—Repeat.

TENSION
7 sts. to 1 inch.
With No. 10 needles cast on 160 sts. and work in K.1, P.1, rib for 1 inch.

NEXT ROW
Rib 20 sts., leave these sts. on a safety pin, rib to end. Slip the first 20 sts. of the next row on to a safety-pin, break off wool and work on the remaining 120 sts. in the following pattern.

1st ROW
X K.2, P.2 rep. from X to end.

2nd ROW
Purl.

Repeat these last two rows for 5½ in., then cast off 36 sts. at the beginning of the next two rows. Continue in pattern on the remaining 48 sts. for a further 5½ in. for the back, ending with the second row of the pattern.

THE NECK BAND
With the right side of work facing, slip the first set of 20 sts. from the pins on to a No. 10 needle, and on to the same needle pick up and knit 52 sts. along the side of the hood. Work in pattern across the 48 sts. of the centre back, then pick up and knit 52 sts. along the other side of the head.
Finally work in rib across the other set of 20 sts. (192 sts.). Work in K.1, P.1, rib for 1½ in., change to No. 12 needles, work 1½ in. in rib, change to No. 10 needles, work 1½ in. in rib. Cast off in the rib.

TO MAKE UP
Press work lightly on wrong side, avoiding ribbing. Sew up the front seam and the two back seams. Press seams.

RADIO ✳ TIMES
JOURNAL OF THE BRITISH BROADCASTING CORPORATION
The war years 1939

'Lies are becoming deadly tedious'

says a member of the BBC's Monitoring Service, after weeks of listening to news and propaganda from all over the world. Here he describes how this war-time activity of the BBC came into being and how it works.

THIS disclosure was made recently in a broadcast talk from Germany by a propagandist only a little less distinguished than Goebbels himself. The speaker was referring, of course, to the 'lies' issued by the British press and wireless, which are a perpetual source of embarrassment to the Nazi Propaganda Ministry, owing to the reputation for truth they enjoy in neutral countries and even in Germany itself.

But like so many observations made by Nazi propagandists, this one can be used as a boomerang; and it is not too fanciful perhaps to detect in it a certain degree of revulsion on the part of the speaker from his daily task of creating new lies with which to justify the Nazi cause.

A local policeman keeps watch over one of the BBC's monitoring posts

New Unit

Certainly the observation expresses perfectly the reaction of a member of the BBC's Monitoring Service after coming off a spell of listening to German news bulletins, talks, and propaganda programmes. Lies *do* become deadly tedious; but it is no good shutting one's ears to them in a war conducted so far mainly by means of propaganda and diplomacy.

And that is why, on the outbreak of war, the BBC, at the request of the Ministry of Information, created a new unit to 'monitor' German transmissions in particular, and transmissions from abroad in general.

The Service then is just over two months old. It inherits from before the war its title, Monitoring—checking either the technical quality or the programme content of a transmission; and a wealth of experience in such work gained over a period of years by BBC engineers, mainly for technical purposes.

The rest has had to be built up during the last ten weeks until today, in every twenty-four hours, something like 150 bulletins in 15 languages are monitored, recorded, translated, summarised, edited, and distributed by the Overseas Intelligence Department of the BBC to the Ministries of State engaged in the prosecution of the war.

As you may imagine the process is a complicated one.

Hogsnorton Again!

It begins in the aerials of a number of receiving stations—one of which is established on a hill overlooking 'Hogsnorton'. The aerials feed a large number of special receiving sets that are tuned in to the stations which it is required to monitor, and the output of them is either recorded or fed by line to a large staff of linguists, who translate into English the words composed by radio news editors and propagandists working in the offices of broadcasting centres all over the world.

The next stage is the transmission by teleprinter of this vast mass of material to the Editing Unit. Here it is carefully and minutely scrutinised.

Then it is passed on to sub-editors who digest, summarise, and put it into a readable form. After that it returns to the night editor who, surveying the whole material for the past twenty-four hours, attempts at four in the morning to write notes on new currents appearing in the stream of propaganda, or on significant news items broadcast, say, from Rome in Arabic or Ankara in French.

Finally, it goes to press, or rather to duplicating, at 8 a.m., to reappear rather miraculously at 11.30 a.m. as the 'Daily Digest of Foreign Broadcasts, Part I, German Transmissions and Daily Notes'; while Part II, 'All Transmissions Other than German', follows at 3 p.m.

The BBC Director-General, Mr. F. W. Ogilvie, (centre, facing camera), visits one of the remote points where foreign programmes are monitored night and day. In the foreground are the machines on which records of particularly interesting broadcasts are made.

So much for the machinery of this new service. It is working at such a speed—three shifts of eight hours each all round the clock and scarcely time for meals—that the human side tends to disappear in a flood of news, propaganda, and counter-propaganda.

The Human Side

But there is a human side, when there is time to think for a moment of items such as that broadcast in Germany recently: 'Only dogs over sixteen inches high will receive an allowance of meat scraps from the butcher's'. Or that by the Dutch announcer who introduced a relay of church bells from Holland for Sweden on All Saints' Day with these words: *May these bells never have to ring for the souls of Dutch and Swedish people who have been forced to lay down their lives in war!*

WE'RE LISTENING...
In a November *RT*, a member of the BBC's Monitoring Service explained how the newly formed unit listened to radio broadcasts from Germany and other countries 24 hours a day and produced daily summaries for "Ministries of State engaged in the prosecution of the war".

JOHN G. WALTER

But we can't advance on Saturday night, sir, we shall miss 'Band Waggon'

JACK MATTHEW

'*When I drive people don't come round corners. It's not done!*'
'To the Public Danger', a story of a car ride by Patrick Hamilton, was one of the most successful broadcasts of this year. It will be repeated tonight at 8.15.

'...and now, if you will just tune down your sets a little...'

GREAT NEWS STORK IS BACK AGAIN !

Same fine nourishment .. *same price*

"**G**IVE us Stork again," said millions of housewives the moment it seemed likely that margarine would be decontrolled. And here is the very news they wanted: you can get Stork now — as much of it as you need!

In spite of difficulties in obtaining exactly the same blend of raw materials for Stork, the makers of this famous margarine have secured the finest ingredients available, have blended them as skilfully as their years of experience have shown them how. So you can be sure of this—though occasionally there must be variations in the actual *blend* of ingredients, the splendid food value of Stork will remain unchanged!

STORK MARGARINE

Contains Sunshine Vitamins A & D

(Gift scheme terminated as previously advertised)

8D per lb.

JS 399-430-65

17

Radio Times, December 8, 1939   Vol. 65   No. 845   Registered at the G.P.O. as a Newspaper

PRICE TWOPENCE

PROGRAMMES FOR
December 10—16

RADIO TIMES

JOURNAL OF THE BRITISH BROADCASTING CORPORATION

(INCORPORATING WORLD-RADIO)

FROM THE MAGINOT LINE

Picture: Gaumont-British News

A feature programme describing the life and work of the French fortress troops on the Western Front which has been recorded in France by Richard Dimbleby and his team of BBC News Observers will be broadcast on Tuesday night.   This picture shows French soldiers on their way to one of the underground entrances to the line.

FRONTLINE NEWS
Richard Dimbleby's report from the Maginot Line in France featured on the front cover in December.

BBC NEWS in SEVENTEEN LANGUAGES

WHEN the listener in Great Britain hears the fading-out of Bow Bells and the familiar voice of the announcer tells him that ' This is the BBC Home Service ', he must often, in spite of the emphasis on the ' Home ', paint to himself an incomplete picture of the work that is being done today by the BBC. I know that until three or four weeks ago that was what I did, and I worked in Broadcasting House.

I won't pretend that I was in total ignorance. Sometimes, in the restaurant, I drank my coffee at the same table as men and women who talked in tongues I couldn't even identify. There was one room in a certain corridor where a small gilt notice-board inscribed with Arabic characters hung on the door, and sometimes I heard of colleagues who had to move out of their offices because foreign-language experts were moving in. Apart from that I couldn't have known less if I had been a solitary inhabitant of St. Kilda.

It all happened very quietly and very quickly, this building up of a wartime overseas service. When I was asked to undertake the preparation of a feature programme describing it for British listeners, I didn't know how much or how little to expect.

Startling Figures

One thing I didn't expect, and that was to be told that today the BBC is broadcasting in seventeen languages. Less than two years ago London was broadcasting only in English. Today there are news services in English, Arabic, French, German, Italian, Spanish and Portuguese (for Europe), Spanish and Portuguese for South America, Afrikaans, Czech, Polish, Greek, Magyar, Rumanian, Serbo-Croat, and Turkish. Another surprise to me was to learn that in the Overseas Service alone forty-nine news bulletins and summaries are broadcast every day, and the number is still increasing.

These figures are evidence of nothing more than rapid development. As I met the men and women who had all the work and anxiety of that development to carry on their shoulders, I began to wonder if there was any way of expressing something of the drama that is implicit in it. There was the drama of swift effort, the battle with time in engaging the right men, momentous nights—such as that of the first broadcast to Germany. There is still the drama of the daily wrestling with the day's news, of the sudden ' breaking ' of an important item of news just as the announcer walks to the microphone, of a single but complicated human effort.

And there is the drama, which one can construct for oneself rather than see, of the reception of the news among once free peoples now under the heel of the oppressor.

PORTUGUESE
Serbo-Croat
German
GREEK
Rumanian
Magyar
Czech
Arabic
TURKISH
SPANISH
French
AFRIKAANS
ITALIAN
Polish

A picture of the BBC Overseas Service will be given to listeners to the BBC Home Service on Sunday, in a programme called ' London Calls the World '. Robert Kemp introduces his programme in this article.

To reflect, as one listens to a bulletin in German, that beyond the Rhine men and women are hearing the same words, in spite of the vigilance of the Gestapo and at the risk of grave penalties, is suddenly to be aware of the grim seriousness which lies behind the bulletins.

The people, too, are a story by themselves. There are the British subjects who control policies and programmes and edit bulletins ; there are men from abroad who speak the bulletins in their mother-tongue and who have it in their power to give valuable advice on the idiom and temper of the bulletins.

In the end I decided to keep my programme as simple and direct as possible, to forget the picturesque frills and the temptation to depict a new Tower of Babel. For Broadcasting House today is the very reverse of the Tower of Babel. There, you remember, confusion reigned. At Broadcasting House, on the other hand, there is continuous co-ordination and dovetailing in the

achievement of one great aim. That aim is the important thing.

I have tried to summarise it by saying that it is the provision of a reliable news service and a statement of the British point of view to the peoples of the world. But even that is inaccurate, for surely the tradition of reliable news which broadcasting has inherited from a free press does itself form part of the British attitude. And these ideals, again, have to be translated into the idiom of the peoples to whom they are addressed.

Empire Backbone

So in Sunday's programme I will begin to tell the story where it began—in the Empire programme which has been serving the Dominions and Colonies since 1932. That is the backbone of the whole thing. Then, in January, 1938, came the Arabic programme, the first of a number of foreign-language services that were added with increasing rapidity as time passed. One of the most exciting moments was the inauguration, at notice of literally a few hours, of the French, German, and Italian services at the time of the Czech crisis. I have had translated into English one of the most effective ' Sonderbericht ' or German ' news-talks ' programmes, that in which Hitler's recorded voice is used to prove the worthlessness of his word, and I hope that listeners will gain from this some idea of what is being done to reach the people inside Germany.

Who Listens ?

Then I will try to describe for you what happens to news from the time it arrives in Broadcasting House on the agency tapes until it goes out in the various languages. Finally, some of the evidence that these broadcasts are widely heard will be presented. For there is an important department which studies in detail the reactions to these bulletins, and they have in their possession many astonishing facts. It is a salutary department, for any broadcaster will tell you that there are moments when he feels himself performing in a vacuum, more cut off from his fellow humans than if he were on Mars, although in point of fact his audience may be numbered in millions.

London Calls the World—and I have thought it worth while to remind those who like to belittle the achievements of their fellow-citizens that the world listens.

The war years 1939

Radio Times (incorporating World-Radio), December 22, 1939

PRICE TWOPENCE

RadioTimes
ChristmasNumber
2ᴅ

A Merry Christmas to all Listeners

J.H.

CHRISTMAS 1939
The first Christmas issue of the Second World War was a morale-boosting exercise in festive bonhomie. AA Thomson's poem *In Spite of All That* (opposite page) with its gentle exhortation to good humour appeared in place of the usual editorial.

In Spite of All That

BY A. A. THOMSON

What do they know of Christmas who only Christmas know
In ordinary peaceful days with robins, cards, and snow—
The careless Christmas of bright lights and sentimental rhyme ;
That gave (if I may coin a phrase) a Dickens of a time ?

That Christmas now has been assaulted all along the line,
And bad old General Black-Out has pursued his dark design ;
There's serious interference with the atmosphere old-fashioned ;
There's even been a rumour that our Christmas may be rationed.

So ponder, O my pessimists, beneath the darkened skies,
On ration-books for turkeys and on coupons for mince-pies.
And would sweet feminine allure survive the cruel blow,
If it had to wear its gas-mask underneath the mistletoe ?

But things are not as bad as that ; let's have it clearly stated :
The spirit of the real thing is not evacuated ;
In spite of all, I promise you that there will be this year
No black-out of benevolence, no censor of good cheer.

The home-fires still keep burning, and, although the trail is long,
The lads go bravely down it with a smile and still a song ;
So long as rabbits run (they say) ; so long as barrels roll,
Nothing can quench their (so to speak) unconquerable soul.

And while, in plaintive harmony, they tell us how they pine
To go and hang their stockings out upon the Siegfried Line,
Let's wish 'em every comfort—turkeys fine and puddings mighty—
That they all could ever hope for, if they'd stayed at home in Blighty.

The hawk-eyed heroes of the air, the sailors of the Fleet,
The wardens who have found this war so hard upon their feet—
May every gallant lad of 'em, on ocean, isle, or isthmus,
Enjoy, without restriction, a completely happy Christmas.

The spirit of our England lives in courage and in laughter ;
In saving what is good and true for those who follow after,
But peace at last will crown the brave, and so, until that day,
God rest you merry, gentlemen, let NOTHING you dismay.

NORMAN MANSBRIDGE

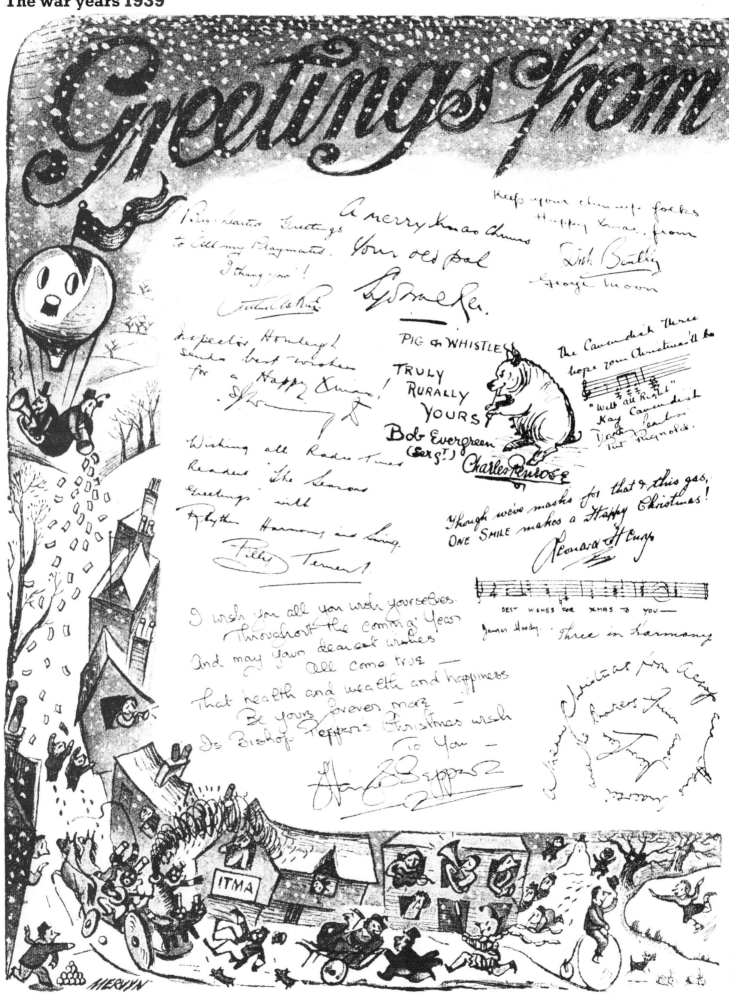

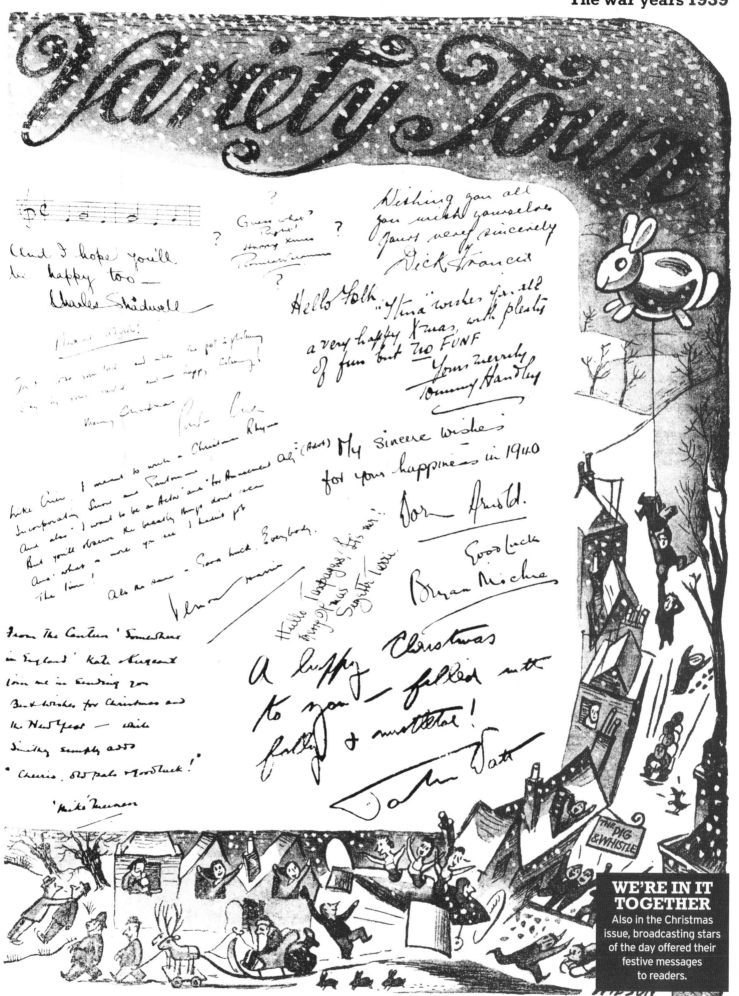

TAKE YOUR CHOICE FROM THE RADIO CHRISTMAS TREE

Christmas Day

RADIO TIMES, ISSUE DATED DECEMBER 22

December 25

767 kc/s 391.1 m. and 668 kc/s 449.1 m.

12.0 noon **FODEN'S MOTOR WORKS BAND**

Conductor, Fred Mortimer

Tone Poem, Coriolanus..................................*Cyril Jenkins*
Xylophone solos by W. Illingworth:
 Splinters..*Illingworth*
 Sparks...*Alford*
Portrait of a Toy Soldier..............................*Ewing*
Selection, The Country Girl............*Monckton and Talbot*

12.30 p.m. **THREE STORIES**

Algernon Blackwood returns to the microphone

A great writer of stories, especially of mystery stories, will be broadcasting three stories of his own today: 'Transition', 'The Laughter of Courage', and 'A Boy and his Bag'. All three were published some years ago. The author has spent a good deal of time on adapting them for radio.

1.0 **Time Signal, Greenwich: NEWS**

1.10 **AN ORCHESTRAL CONCERT**

Conducted by Guy Warrack

Overture, The Vale of Love.............................*Oscar Straus*
Suite, Children's Games—1 March, Trumpet and Drum. 2 Berceuse, The Doll. 3 Impromptu, The Top. 4 Duo, Little Husband, Little Wife. 5 Galop, The Ball...*Bizet*
Rhapsody, España.....................................*Chabrier*

1.35 **'THE SOLDIER SINGS'**

A programme of national and popular songs in contemporary settings, devised and written by Dr. Thomas Wood

The programme is in six scenes

1—The Spanish Armada ; 2 The Civil War ; 3—The Great Rebellion ; 4—Waterloo ; 5—The Crimea ; 6—1914-1918

The incidents used have been based on fact so far as fact could be established

The cast includes: Alan Howland, James McPhee, Francis de Wolff, Beryl Laverick, Clifford Bean, Cameron Hall, Howard Marion-Crawford, Albert Ward

with the BBC Men's Chorus (Chorus master, Leslie Woodgate) and the BBC Military Band, conducted by P. S. G. O'Donnell

Production by Felix Felton and Maurice Brown

'The Soldier Sings' shows in their historical settings some of the most famous tunes in the history of the British nation, from 'Lord Willoughby', which was sung when Queen Elizabeth reviewed her troops before the Armada, to the songs sung in a Divisional concert-party hut in France in the last war.

Today's programme is a revised form of the programme originally broadcast in May, 1938.

AT THREE O'CLOCK

A MESSAGE TO THE EMPIRE FROM

HIS MAJESTY THE KING

following

2.15 **THE EMPIRE'S GREETING**

Christmas scenes and Christmas greetings between the peoples of the Commonwealth

The peoples of the British Commonwealth are at war. On this day of reunion by radio in 'one great family' they meet again in battle-dress

Narrator, Howard Marshall. Producer, Laurence Gilliam

Christmas with the Forces :

The Royal Navy: The Dover Patrol
The Army: The British Expeditionary Force
The Royal Air Force: The Fighter Command

HIS MAJESTY

THE KING

will broadcast a message to

the Empire this afternoon at

3.0—following

THE EMPIRE'S GREETING

a reunion by radio of the peoples

of the Commonwealth (2.15-3.0)

KING'S SPEECH
The radio listings for Christmas Day 1939, including the address to the British Empire at 3pm by King George VI.

RADIO TIMES
JOURNAL OF THE BRITISH BROADCASTING CORPORATION
The war years 1940

1940

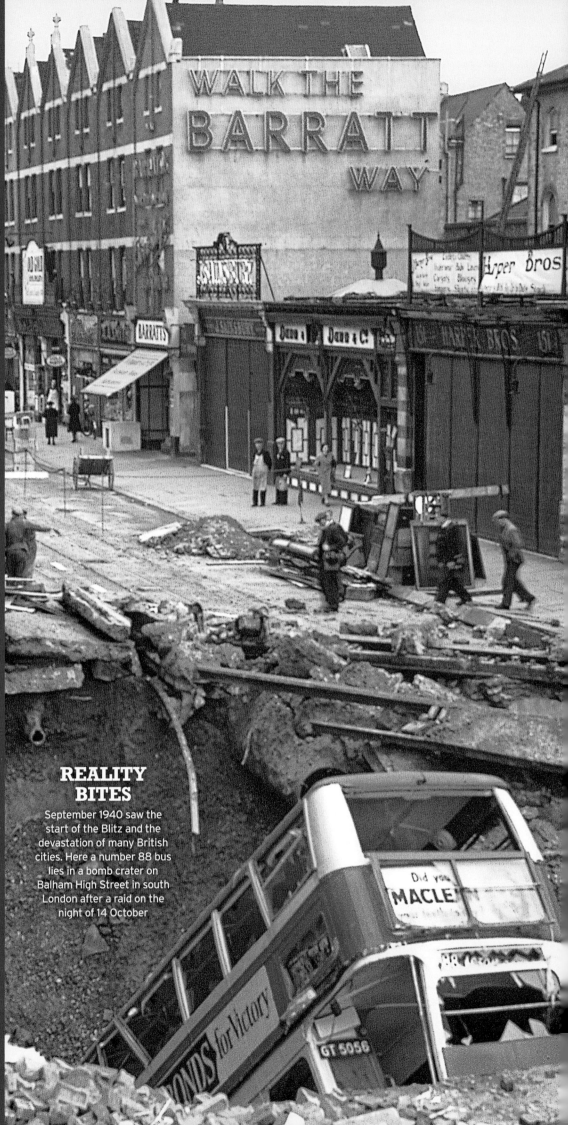

REALITY BITES

September 1940 saw the start of the Blitz and the devastation of many British cities. Here a number 88 bus lies in a bomb crater on Balham High Street in south London after a raid on the night of 14 October

Radio Times, December 29, 1939 Vol. 66 No. 848 Registered at the G.P.O. as a Newspaper

PROGRAMMES FOR
Dec. 31—Jan. 6

PRICE TWOPENCE

RADIO TIMES
JOURNAL OF THE BRITISH BROADCASTING CORPORATION
(INCORPORATING WORLD-RADIO)

Arthur Askey

is being Big-Hearted in pantomime now. You will hear him from the stage of the Prince of Wales Theatre, Birmingham, on Wednesday.

ALSO THIS WEEK:

'For Auld Lang Syne'
A Scrapbook of Scrapbooks

Will Fyffe
from Somewhere in France

Carl Brisson
in 'Monday Night at Eight'

Return of

Café Colette

'Wings over Ruritania'
a sequel to 'The Merry Princess'

'Mother Goose'
from Bradford

'Dangerous Corner'
J. B. Priestley's play

Star attractions

As the calendar turned to January 1940, Arthur Askey, Robert Donat and a range of sports were lined up to entertain listeners. Look closer at these covers and you'll also see appearances from Will Fyffe, Prime Minister Neville Chamberlain, George Formby and Mother Goose...

'How to bring Britain to its knees..?

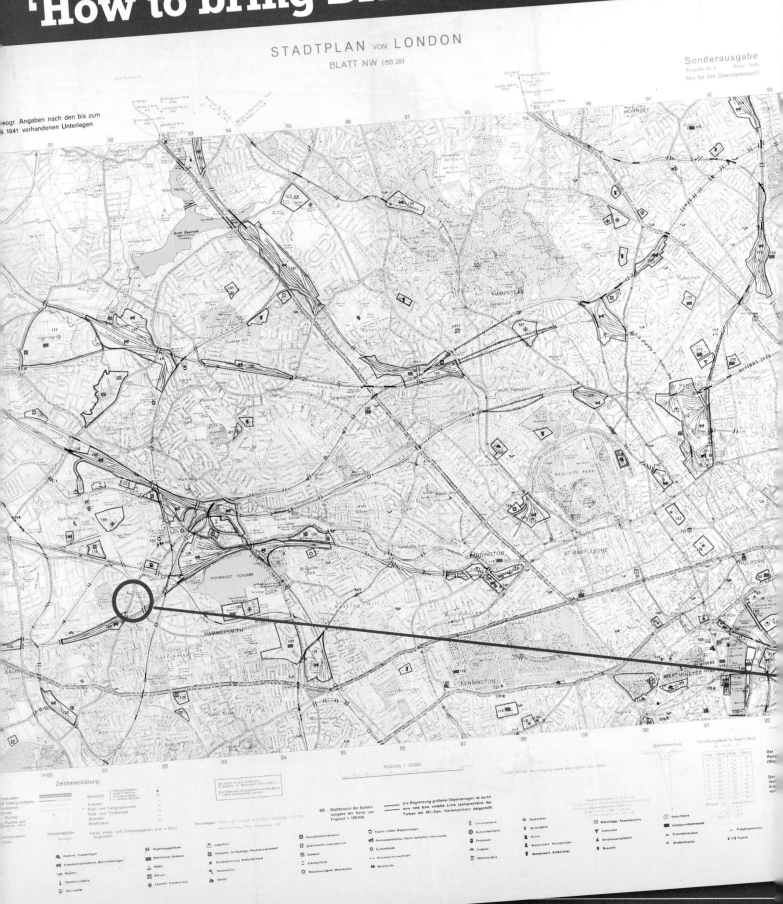

STADTPLAN VON LONDON
BLATT NW (BB 29)

Destroy *Radio Times*!'

When war was declared, the BBC moved its operations from Broadcasting House in central London to Wood Norton near Evesham in Worcestershire. *Radio Times* followed suit. While the editor, Maurice Gorham, remained at Broadcasting House, staff were evacuated to the safety of the Waterlows print works at Park Royal in north-west London.

Little did the BBC know that the Luftwaffe had earmarked the site as a potential target. This was confirmed after the war, when maps and photographs identifying Waterlows were found at Luftwaffe headquarters in Berlin. The Germans would have known all about the importance of the BBC to the British war effort and to morale in the event of war, and the embassy staff in London would have explained the part *Radio Times* played in that. So while they couldn't bomb the BBC off the air, the Germans could certainly try to deprive the British people of a copy of *Radio Times*.

Production of the magazine became hazardous during the Blitz, and Gorham was visiting the plant when German bombers struck. He wrote, "We were nearly all of us in the trench shelters when Waterlows was bombed. Two of the canteen staff were not, and I had the experience I had always imagined and never really expected – running out to give a hand with the casualties and then returning to the shelter and going on passing the page proofs."

The Luftwaffe *Stadtplan* (far left) and German aerial photograph (below) showing Waterlows, the print works specially built for the production of *Radio Times* (left)

GB 12, BB 29, Nr. 171: Waterlow's Großdruckerei in Park Royal (West London).
Großdruckerei der Radio Times.

It was on the Luftwaffe List

This photograph, taken from German air force files in Berlin, shows that the Waterlow plant, on which the "Radio Times" is produced, was scheduled for destruction. It was damaged, but only slightly.

Radio Times, January 26, 1940   Vol. 66   No. 852   Registered at the G.P.O. as a Newspaper

PRICE TWOPENCE

PROGRAMMES FOR
Jan. 28—Feb. 3

RADIO ✳ TIMES
JOURNAL OF THE BRITISH BROADCASTING CORPORATION
(INCORPORATING WORLD-RADIO)

FXD 179

BBC

THE BBC AT THE FRONT

The recording unit with the B.E.F. in France is now presenting a regular Saturday-night despatch from the Western Front. Here is the unit in action with a hand microphone. See the article by Richard Dimbleby (centre, above) on page 5.

With the BBC at the Front

From RICHARD DIMBLEBY and Co., whose regular weekly despatches from France start tomorrow (Saturday) at 6.15

c/o Directorate of Public Relations,
G.H.Q., B.E.F.

January, 1940.

DEAR EDITOR,

YOU asked us to write to you as soon as we could, giving some idea of what we've been doing here since we came out.

Well, we started in October by keeping a careful record of our activities, but lately it seems to have gone rather astray. However, our diaries, such as they are, show that we've inflicted on listeners about thirty special reports, one longer programme (the Maginot Line), more than half a dozen concerts or Variety shows, and a dozen or so ' special ' items, mostly around Christmas. Also we've been able to do some work with the American and French radio, and we have established a close liaison with the latter. In most of our reports officers and men themselves have spoken ; we hope listeners will agree that so far we have succeeded in acting as some sort of a link between the Army here and its families at home. That is the chief justification for our presence here.

Taking the Records to Bed

Conditions here as a whole have been reasonable, although recently the weather became troublesome. We reached a stage when we skidded wildly about on icy roads all day and all night. Sarney, as engineer-in-chief, had to share his bed with the discs to prevent their freezing. Incidentally, if you hear any hissing in our recorded reports, it isn't us, but just a record that's been got at by Jack Frost in spite of Sarney's self-sacrifice. Christmas Day was the worst of all.

I don't think we told you anything of the background of our Christmas broadcasts—how the medical corps speakers in the ' Empire Greeting ' programme arrived thirty seconds before they spoke, having given First Aid at two road accidents on the way ; how the Deputy Chaplain-General lost a wing and a bumper before arriving at the service ; or, for that matter, how half the competitors in the spelling bee and Jack Payne and his band just didn't arrive at all.

Nor did you hear about Dimbleby's drive back from the Maginot Line on Christmas Eve after fixing the details of the French troop concert there. It seems to have rivalled Tschiffely's. It took fifteen and a half hours, most of it sideways, and ended here at our headquarters at two o'clock on Christmas morning.

What with one thing and another, there were some bad moments, but we managed to get away with it all, and rewarded ourselves with a day off.

However, we haven't been as heroic as we expected. There's been more discomfort than danger. We can say for ourselves that we haven't missed an opportunity of getting to the business end of things. We have been near enough to German soldiers to distinguish their features, if that conveys anything to you, and we've seen artillery and aircraft in action. Once when we were in a French advance post someone in the other front line fired five rifle shots, and we spent some time arguing whether he was shooting at us. If so, he missed. But this will seem very trivial to older campaigners than ourselves.

We're glad to report that the faithful recording car is still going strong in spite of a good many vicissitudes, including a sudden meeting with a French car and a wall at 50 m.p.h. Entente or no, it was the Frenchman's fault. Nobody was hurt, nor was the recording gear, but the car was laid up for ten days, and we had to hire one and borrow another from our opposite numbers in the French State Radio.

We made several resolutions for the new year, but how many we can keep depends naturally on general events. If possible, we shall keep up the supply of reports for the news

The BBC unit : (L. to R.) the recording car, Dimbleby, Sarney, the conducting officer of the unit; and Howarth

bulletins, and in addition we are starting on January 27 a weekly series of despatches which will be broadcast on Saturdays from 6.15 to 6.30 p.m. In these we intend to deal with the aspects of the Army's work which need more detailed description than one can fit into the shorter news periods. There are the Army Services, for example, which have not yet seen much of the limelight, and there are many picturesque units of the French army whose work would interest British listeners.

More Concert Broadcasts

We shall arrange more Variety and concert broadcasts direct from the zone, and we hope to be able to give a chance to some of the amateur talent here as well as to ENSA stars. Howarth, who calls himself the maid-of-all-work of the party (as indeed he is), has taken unto himself the job of listening to concert parties in all parts of the British area, and we intend to put our seven or eight best discoveries into one really good troop broadcast.

All this rests on the assumption that ' the situation ' remains much as it is. If the balloon goes up, our plans go with it. But we think we have laid things on well enough—to use an Army term—to keep some sort of channel open to London for bare news reports, whatever happens. More than that we cannot say !

Yours sincerely,

Richard Dimbleby

David Howarth

H. F. Sarney

P.S.—Could you find a way of telling all the people who have been sending us ' comforts ' for the Army that we're quite happy to pass them on ? Sometimes when we get a day or two behind, our attic studio-cum-office looks like one of those village shops that sell everything, but we can assure people that everything goes to someone who needs it.

One other thing: We should be glad to have the comments, rude or otherwise, of anyone who has time to write to us out here about our programmes.

An A.A. battery ' somewhere in France ' records a programme for listeners at home

REPORTS FROM FRANCE

This issue marked the launch of a weekly radio despatch from France by Richard Dimbleby (centre, wearing an overcoat). He had been with the British Expeditionary Force since October 1939 and wrote: "We hope listeners will agree that so far we have succeeded in acting as some sort of a link between the Army here and its families at home." He also noted in a breezy style an epic car journey through snow and ice, "most of it sideways", meeting troops and being shot at from the German front line.

AN 'ITMA' WHO'S WHO

All good things must come to an end, and 'Itma', whose weekly Tuesdays are now numbered, is no exception. So this is the time to take you behind the scenes to meet the boys and girls who have made Funf and the Office of Twerps a hilarious reality in millions of homes (we wish we had as many shillings).

TOMMY HANDLEY, chief funmaker in the notorious Office of Twerps, was born in Liverpool. After leaving school, he entered a corn merchant's, where, so he says, he 'learned to flick corn with incredible accuracy at adjacent office windows'. Here, too, he probably picked up some of his ideas for the running of the 'Itma' office. Made his BBC début fifteen years ago in a series of revues, and has been a top-liner ever since.

Off-stage he is very much as he is in the studio—full of staccato wisecracks, with a good line in far-fetched puns, and an ability to keep his face straight when those around are convulsed.

When the war broke out Tommy was one of the original members of the BBC's Bristol expeditionary force and was the first BBC artist to put over a wartime song hit—'Who is this man who looks like Charlie Chaplin?', composed by John Watt and Max Kester.

In private life a simple soul who likes nothing better in his spare time than to stroll round Clifton Zoo with a bag of jelly babies in one pocket and a bag of nuts in the other. The babies are for himself and the bag of nuts for himself and the monkeys. Tommy likes bananas too, and that's why he can't bear to see his favourite animal fed—Alfred, an out-size in gorillas, gulps down forty of them at a sitting.

* * * *

VERA LENNOX plays the part of Dotty, Tommy Handley's 'Itma' secretary. The thing troubling her at the moment is that she's running out of misnomers for Tommy—there's a limit to the variations on Mr. Handcuff, Mr. Handbasin, Mr. Handbell, etc.

She began her stage career at the age of ten in *The Swineherd and the Princess*, and has since starred in almost everything, from Wodehouse farce to Shakespeare. The trouper tradition comes naturally to her. The show's the thing, whatever she feels like. A fortnight ago she had such a bad cold that Dotty's boo-hoos were accompanied by a stream of tears.

As well as Dotty, Vera portrays in 'Itma' any exotic woman who may be in the script—Helga Schwenk, the beautiful spy, for instance, was her creation.

* * * *

JACK TRAIN, regularly plays three parts—Fusspot, old Jollop, and, last but not least, the fearful Funf. Funf first made his appearance in the second 'Itma' broadcast of the war. It was a characteristic début.

Funf: This is Funf speaking.

Handley: Funf ? Funf ? Is that a name or a rude expression ?

Funf: It is Funf, your favourite spy.

Funf was Worsley's idea—the origin of the character was recently described by 'The Broadcasters' in the RADIO TIMES. The master-stroke was also Worsley's invention—to make Funf's sinister tones reverberate in a tumbler. Jack is now so used to Funfing into a tumbler that he

can't drink a glass of beer without blowing bubbles—that's what Tommy Handley says, anyway.

Apart from Fusspot and Jollop, Jack can twist his voice about so much that he can impersonate almost anybody he feels inclined to. He is slight, dapper, lean, with dark hair that keeps its shiny neatness until he gives an impersonation of Hitler. Another thing that spoils his appearance is his Lionel Barrymore imitation—all his suits show signs of wear round the lapels, which he clutches in true Barrymore fashion.

His first broadcast was from Plymouth in the very early days of 5PY. His act consisted of a couple of songs and a tune on the banjolele. 'You sang beautifully, Jack', said a friend the following morning, 'but the fellow who strummed the banjolele couldn't play for nuts.'

He has done quite, a lot of straight acting, notably in *Journey's End* in the West End and on tour. Funf is his favourite part, however, the only snag being that he finds it difficult not to laugh. Listen carefully and you may hear a snigger or two escape from the tumbler.

* * * *

MAURICE DENHAM plays Mrs. Tickle, Vodkin, and Ferdinand, announcer of Radio Fakenburg. In addition to the quavering falsetto of the glamorous Lola Tickle (studio audiences invariably murmur in surprise: 'Well, I never! It's a man!'), Maurice can sing and speak tenor, contralto, bass, soprano, and baritone.

His hair has retreated rather prematurely from his forehead, making him look older than he is ; actually, he is only just thirty.

Made his radio début in February, 1938. At the outbreak of war he had well over a hundred broadcasts to his credit. Additional appearances since then must have sent his total up to the 250 mark. He has done character in radio, from being the Rabbit in 'Winnie the Pooh' and reading stories in schools broadcasts, to playing Reggie Neemo in all the 'Mr. and Mrs. Neemo' sketches, and Gabby in *Gulliver's Travels*. He also acted the baby for Arthur Askey's foundling in 'Band Waggon', so expertly that there were several accusations of cruelty and dark talk about reports to the N.S.P.C.C.

The rôle he likes best in 'Itma' is helping with the 'effects', particularly if it's something messy like water, but best of all he can supply the cries of pigs and fowls.

* * * *

BILLY TERNENT has provided the music for 'Itma' ever since the outbreak of war. The band started by doing an ordinary accompanying job, and has now developed into an integral part of the show—they can put down their instruments and do a cross-talk act with Tommy Handley.

'Itma' has already got under the skin of the band boys. They laugh as much as the audience, which is very rare for a band, and altogether behave rather peculiarly. Studio audiences, unacquainted with the wild effects 'Itma' has

on those taking part in it, look quite worried when the boys give Red Indian shrieks at the end of the broadcast.

Billy is the Beau Brummell of the 'Itma' outfit—a lithe figure, faultlessly dressed, with hair that looks like an advertisement for Persico Brilliantine. For more than thirteen years he has been attached to Jack Hylton. Despite travels all over the world in tours with Hylton, you can still hear Billy's native town in his speech—Newcastle.

No, he didn't compose the 'Itma' signature tune. This catchy little number was put together by Francis Worsley and Michael North. The 'commercial' tune, which Sam Costa sings to different words every week in the Radio Fakenburg 'spot', is the work of a BBC Variety producer, Leslie Bridgmont.

* * * *

THE CAVENDISH THREE are the young ladies who, among other things, introduce 'Itma' with the 'It's That Man Again' signature tune and make Tommy Handley's office life difficult by acting as auxiliary secretaries to Vera Lennox.

Two of them, Kay Cavendish and Pat Rignold, have dark brown hair, the third, Dorothy Carless, is a blonde. All are tall and attractive.

* * * *

SAM COSTA is not only the vocalist, but Lemuel, that 'common boy' who worries Tommy Handley with 'Five, five, five', etc. 'Itma' has turned him into an actor. The 'common boy' act worries him. If it gets a hold on him, he thinks, he might never again be able to croon rhymes like 'day' and 'say' without turning them to 'dye' and 'sigh'. Twenty-nine-year-old Sam does his funny stuff with a gusto worthy of a red-nosed comic, yet takes his singing seriously. When he croons, he pleads so realistically to the microphone that it is said his wife becomes jealous. Comes of a musical family that included Michael Costa, a conductor well known round about the middle of the nineteenth century. Apart from his singing, he has held down jobs in first-class dance bands on his merits as a pianist.

* * * *

TED KAVANAGH writes the scripts. You were told all about him and the weekly 'Itma' sit-round, where the ideas are hatched, in a RADIO TIMES article by Harold Rathbone two weeks ago.

* * * *

FRANCIS WORSLEY, producer, is, in his own words, 'not really a producer at all, but an administrator'. After coming down from Oxford in 1926, he went to the Gold Coast as an education officer looking after a bush province about the size of Wales, but was invalided out of the Civil Service eighteen months after. He joined the BBC as a talks assistant at Cardiff in 1928, and had an interim of looking after outside broadcasts and being programme director of the West Region before he was attached to the Variety department a year ago. The thing that he's most proud of is that he has played cricket for Glamorgan on several occasions.

When 'Itma' started four weeks before war was declared—Tommy Handley had a floating broadcasting station in those days—Worsley had a worrying time choosing a title for the show. It was very nearly christened MUG — the Ministry of Universal Gratification.

For a man who can create and enjoy slapstick humour, Worsley has a large serious streak in his make-up. He can prove in a few words how 'Itma' follows the old traditions of the morality play and pantomime. Tommy Handley is Noah, Vodkin is Mrs. Noah, and Funf is Beelzebub, a power of evil made funny.

The artists who work with him swear by him.

ITMA ITMA ITMA

TOMMY'S TEAM

In January 1940, *Radio Times* revealed the faces behind *It's That Man Again* (*ITMA*), the famous radio comedy starring Tommy Handley (above). The show was a highlight in the war years and beyond. It ran until 1949 and ended when Handley died at the age of 56.

'Mother's pride and joy, Mrs. Handley's boy'

BEHIND THE SCENES: Each week's 'Itma' broadcast is thrashed out over the teacups by (L. to R.) Francis Worsley, Tommy Handley, Ted Kavanagh, Jack Train, and Maurice Denham

MEANWHILE THE BAND WILL PLAY . . . and on the left is Billy Ternent, who conducts it, and is an integral part of the 'Itma' outfit

WHAT A COMMON BOY!—Sam Costa, vocalist, now adds to the weekly complications as Lemuel, the adenoidal office-boy

. . . VOUS POUVEZ CRACHER!—Maurice Denham puts his heart into blowing the pip-pip signal of Radio Fakenburg

THIS IS FUNF SPEAKING—and this is exactly how Jack Train does it. Jack is also, when necessary, Funf's Father and Funf's Grandfather!

WELL, ALL RIGHT, ALL RIGHT! — (Left) Tommy with his secretaries. Vera Lennox, as Dotty, (Oh, Mr. Handcuff!), is seated, and the Cavendish Three are behind.

MOST IRREGULAR! — On the right is Mrs. Tickle (Maurice Denham) herself, complete with mop, doing her best for one of her gentlemen, in this case Jack Train, as Fusspot—or Jollop—or both!

Radio Times, February 16, 1940   Vol. 66   No. 855   Registered at the G.P.O. as a Newspaper

PRICE TWOPENCE

PROGRAMMES FOR
February 18—24

8

RADIO TIMES

JOURNAL OF THE BRITISH BROADCASTING CORPORATION

(INCORPORATING WORLD-RADIO)

FOR THE FORCES

The twelve-hour daily programmes start this week

The service of special programmes intended for men of the Navy, Army, and Air Force is being extended to twelve hours daily, from 11 a.m. to 11 p.m. Full details of all programmes are now given in the RADIO TIMES side by side with details of the Home Service programmes. Information about the new service will be found on page 3.

FOR THE FORCES

This February edition marked the start of the BBC's For the Forces schedule for those serving in the Navy, Army and Air Force, which ran daily for 12 hours a day starting at 11.00am. The new programmes were aimed at squads of "at least half-a-dozen men grouped round one loudspeaker", rather than "a single listener sitting in solitary concentration by his own fireside".

RADIO TIMES
FULL-TIME PROGRAMMES
FOR THE FORCES

TURN to the programme pages this week, and you will find a change. The Home Service programmes have had to squeeze up to make room for a welcome bedfellow in the shape of the programmes intended for listeners in His Majesty's Forces, sailors, soldiers, and airmen on active service both at home and abroad.

There have been programmes for the Forces since January 7 from 6.0 p.m. onwards, and a summary of the items to be broadcast on the extra wavelength during the evening hours have duly appeared in the RADIO TIMES. But with the inauguration this Sunday, February 18, of a full twelve-hour service, from 11.0 a.m. to 11.0 p.m., the items will now be printed in as full detail as the Home Service programmes are. Actually this arrangement, paradoxically enough, allows more room not only for complete details of each programme but for more of those supplementary annotations which have been for over ten years a feature of our programme pages.

When the evening programmes for the Forces now being broadcast were first introduced it was stated in the RADIO TIMES: 'This is an experiment. If it succeeds, the BBC hopes soon to present the troops with something much more complete in the way of a daily programme.' Well, the experiment *has* succeeded. Technical difficulties have been overcome, and the requirements of national security (still the first thing to be considered) have not been infringed.

Meanwhile the BBC has been conducting a systematic inquiry into what kind of programmes are most likely to satisfy those for whom this service is intended. All kinds of evidence has already been received from officers and men of the Navy, Army, and Air Force. And the first full-time programmes have been planned on the basis of what they have had to say. You will probably recall that the Director-General of the BBC has himself visited France to try to ascertain at first hand the likes and dislikes of the British Expeditionary Force and the Royal Air Force in France in particular. You will have heard his broadcast on February 7. You will have learned of his discovery that there seems to be the prospect of as much difficulty in satisfying all tastes in France as there has always notoriously been in satisfying all the different tastes of listeners at home.

* * * *

Nevertheless various general assumptions have been made. One is that most active-service listening will be group listening.

TIMES AND WAVELENGTHS

The full twelve-hour service of BBC programmes for the Forces will be heard this week on the following wavelengths:

11 a.m. to 6 p.m.	373.1 m., 804 kc/s only
6 p.m. to 7 p.m. {	373.1 m., 804 kc/s 342.1 m., 877 kc/s
7 p.m. to 11 p.m.	342.1 m., 877 kc/s only

NOTE—With the coming of British Summer Time on February 25 the above times, though not the wavelengths, will be slightly changed. Details of the changes will be given in next week's RADIO TIMES.

That is to say, the picture that the programme planners have in mind is of at least half-a-dozen men grouped round one loudspeaker rather than of a single listener sitting in solitary concentration by his own fireside. A second safe assumption, arising out of the first, is that light programmes will always be more acceptable, the kind of programmes that do not suffer unduly by interruption, either by conversation or by the call of duty — indeed, the kind of programmes that may even be enhanced by communal enjoyment and a running exchange of comment.

Thus the BBC offers to this special audience of listeners plenty of Variety entertainment, both from the studio and from theatres ; of dance-band programmes (from France as well as from Britain) ; of theatre-organ broadcasts, both from St. George's Hall and from cinemas where leading artists play ; and outside broadcasts from theatres of excerpts from musical shows and revues.

There will be radio thrillers, community singing, students' songs, and all possible kinds of sports broadcasts as they come along. One particular sports broadcast of special interest should awaken the eager anticipation of the Canadian troops : this is the recording for half-an-hour every Sunday evening of a commentary from Canada on the best of the previous day's ice hockey games.

Talks will be few. They will include two weekly talks on sport, on Thursdays and Saturdays, when well-known sportsmen will be broadcasting. On Tuesdays that very human speaker John Hilton will talk about activities on the home front. Also on Tuesdays, every other week, there will be a fortnightly report, a kind of news-letter, from the Navy and Air Force, to keep the Army informed of what the other two Services are doing and how they are faring. Finally, there is 'Close Up', a feature that will cover all news of the world of entertainment.

In response to an already considerable demand there will be simple and entertainingly-devised lessons in French twice a week.

Each day's broadcast will open with a summary of the programmes to be heard during the day, and will close with a similar summary for the following day.

* * * *

The point to emphasise about all these plans is that they are still tentative and experimental. The BBC cannot, any more than any other organisation, lay claims yet to expert knowledge of what exactly constitutes 'the stuff to give the troops'. Only the troops themselves are able to reveal that. Even the experience of entertainers twenty-five years ago can be no guide to what the new generation of sailors, soldiers, and airmen prefers, a generation of civilian fighters who have come to maturity in a world in which the new popular arts of radio and the films have helped to mould public taste anew.

So the BBC awaits the verdict of the men of the fighting forces, and it cordially invites that verdict. Please, if you are a member of His Majesty's Forces, listen to the programmes, then write to the BBC with your opinions, criticisms, and suggestions ; and in this way there may be every hope that a service which is now experimental shall be quickly strengthened into one of proven value.

Invitation to all who are serving with H.M. Forces at home, on the sea, or abroad : the BBC will be delighted to receive letters from you with your opinions, criticisms, and suggestions in connection with the special programmes intended for your entertainment. It is anxious for *your* collaboration in making these programmes a real success. Please write to the BBC.

BRITISH EXPEDITIONARY FORCE EDITIONS

For the troops

With the British Expeditionary Force stationed in France awaiting action, in 1940 *Radio Times* began printing alternative editions for the BEF at a price of 1.50 francs. The covers often featured photographs of the glamorous female stars of the day like *Hi, Gang!*'s Bebe Daniels, Elizabeth Allan and the original Eliza Doolittle, Wendy Hiller.

Radio Times, May 24, 1940 Vol. 67 No. 869 Registered at the G.P.O. as a Newspaper

FRANCS 1.50

PROGRAMMES FOR
May 26—June 1

RADIO ✻ TIMES
JOURNAL OF THE BRITISH BROADCASTING CORPORATION
BRITISH EXPEDITIONARY FORCE EDITION

★ Bebe ★
DANIELS
is in the new Sunday show,
★ 'Hi, Gang!' with ★
VIC OLIVER
and
BEN LYON
★

Three of America's finest comedy artists are to entertain you regularly in this new Variety series.
Bebe Daniels (she pronounces it Beebee), Harold Lloyd's leading lady in films at the age of fourteen, and star of the memorable *Rio Rita* . . . a beautiful face, as you see here, and a glorious singing voice, as you will hear on Sunday.
Ben Lyon, her husband and partner, now appearing with her in the revue *Haw-Haw* at the Holborn Empire . . . leapt to fame in the film *Hell's Angels* . . .

Radio Times, April 5 1940 Vol. 67 No. 862 Registered at the G.P.O. . . .

FRANCS 1.50

PROGRAMMES FOR
April 7—13

RADIO ✻ TIMES
JOURNAL OF THE BRITISH BROADCASTING CORPORATION
BRITISH EXPEDITIONARY FORCE EDITION

ELIZABETH ALLAN
beautiful star of the British stage and screen will be interviewed in 'Close-Up' on Monday

SUNDAY this week, will be an outstanding day in a bright week for B.E.F. listeners.
Make a point of listening, if you can, to three gay shows. First comes a broadcast from Regent, a cheery Variety concert, with Bennett and Williams, Beryl Orde, Ted Ray, Bettie Bucknelle, and Leonard Henry as the stars. This is early in the afternoon.
Later in the afternoon you will hear something of the great Jazz Jamboree at the Gaumont State, Kilburn, another cheery affair, with a bevy of the best dance orchestras going through their paces. The bands you will hear are those of Oscar Rabin, Ken Johnson, Jack Harris, Maurice Winnick, and Geraldo—representing every style of orchestration and presentation. Christopher Stone will act in compère.
Finally, in the evening, Tommy Handley, Harold Bottrss, Patricia Rossborough, and Eddie Carroll and Jan Ralzel will broadcast from the Palladium in an all-star concert organised by the National Sunday League.
All this in addition to the usual favourite Sunday features—the mixture performance of 'Garrison Theatre', Doris Arnold's 'These You Have Loved', and a half-hour of Sandy Macpherson.
Who said Sunday broadcasting was dull ?

Radio Times, March 8, 1940 Vol. 66 No. 858 Registered at the G.P.O. as a Newspaper

PRICE FRANCS 1.50

PROGRAMMES FOR
March 10—16

RADIO ✻ TIMES
JOURNAL OF THE BRITISH BROADCASTING CORPORATION
BRITISH EXPEDITIONARY FORCE EDITION

Wendy Hiller

will be one of the stars interviewed by Leslie Mitchell in 'Close-Up' on Monday

*T*his is Wendy Hiller. She is the young actress who made such a hit in the title rôle of 'Pygmalion' just over a year ago. Her study of the bedraggled Cockney slum girl who changed into a creature so gorgeous that she nearly deceived us was so extraordinary that even the dourest United States critics put it third in the list of the ten best film performances of 1939.
From her lips, the victorious adjective dropped with just as much the effect of a bombshell as when the great Mrs. Patrick Campbell first uttered it in the stage production of 'Pygmalion' a quarter of a century earlier. And how the audience rocked!
Wendy started her acting career at the Manchester Repertory Theatre less than ten years ago. She burst upon London three months less than five years later, making a hit in the tragic Lancashire heroine of 'Love on the Dole'. She repeated this success in New York the following year.
Then came a revival of Shaw's play 'Saint Joan' at the Malvern Festival, and Shaw himself picked Wendy to take the principal part. From that it was only a step to 'Pygmalion', on both stage and screen, and to the second big Shaw film, 'Major Barbara' which is now in production, and in which Wendy is again to play the title rôle, and will wear a Salvation Army bonnet.

Radio Times, April 12, 1940   Vol. 67   No. 863   Registered at the G.P.O. as a Newspaper

PROGRAMMES FOR
April 14—20

FRANCS 1.50

RADIO ✳ TIMES
JOURNAL OF THE BRITISH BROADCASTING CORPORATION

BRITISH EXPEDITIONARY FORCE EDITION

Gracie Fields

is here again! On Tuesday you will be able to hear her broadcasting from the Paris Opera House in a special all-star, Anglo-French concert.

★ ★ ★ ★ ★ ★ ★ ★ ★ ★

GRACIE! Our Gracie! She can do anything with an audience, whether they see her or only hear her. She can make you split your sides with laughter, then in a moment she can bore through your tunic to touch your most sentimental spot and make your eyes moist. She can get a whole crowd of you singing rollicking choruses at the tops of your voices, then a minute later you can sit back quietly and be thrilled by her liquid notes as she sings 'Ave Maria' or 'Jerusalem' —or, as in her Christmas Day broadcast, 'O come, all ye faithful'.

Above all, the secret of Gracie's enchantment is her sympathy. As you listen to her, you know very well that she has great sympathetic imagination. You feel instinctively that she knows how bored you can get with cleaning your buttons and all the other hundred-and-one dreary routine duties.

She knows it all. She is not one of your condescending high-hat sort, but one of the people—one of you!

Is it too much to hail her, as all her soldier, sailor, and airmen audiences hail her of the boys'?

AWAY AND HOME
The cover of the British Expeditionary Force edition for 14–20 April 1940 featured Forces' Sweetheart Gracie Fields. Back in Britain, the standard edition (right) depicted the flying-boats of the RAF Coastal Command patrolling Britain's vital sea routes.

'What infernal noise is that in there?'
'Programme for the Forces, Sir.'

'HELTER-SHELTER'. Come and join the cheerful shelterers tonight at 8.0 when a new Variety show for the Home Front gets going.

'Now in a second or two, all being well, you people at home will hear the shell actually leaving the gun'

HOW TO HANDLE YOUR DOG IN AN AIR RAID

Panic measures are entirely unnecessary, and provided you take a few simple precautions, your dog can continue to give you his faithful companionship in these difficult times of war.

1 Install your dog's sleeping basket in the air raid shelter or refuge room and let him get accustomed to sleeping there.

2 To minimise fear and reduce shock give the dog a dose of Bob Martin's Fit and Hysteria Powders when the raid warning sounds. They cost only 6d. a carton from all chemists and dog-food shops.

3 If your dog is of an excitable nature and is inclined to snap at strangers, it would be an advisable safeguard to keep a muzzle handy. Glide the muzzle *gently* into position — don't tug it!

4 Avoid undue agitation when handling the dog. *Keep Calm* — and your dog will be made less 'nervy' by your example. Your calm will be a reassurance to him — his company will comfort you.

☞ Detailed instructions on air raid protection and wartime care of dogs and cats are contained in a special booklet 'Your Dog and Cat in Wartime.' Every owner is urged to write for a free copy from Bob Martin Ltd., 98 Union St., Southport, Lancs.

BOMBERS OVER GERMANY

In an issue from August, *RT* shone a light on the role being played by RAF bomber pilots. The billing for *Bombers over Germany* said: "Listeners will be told exactly what happened from the moment the Whitley bombers took off, to the moment they landed after their trip to Bremen." The trip in question was a bombing raid on an oil refinery.

YOUR WARTIME FOOD

This food chart is issued in connection with the Tuesday-morning talks, 'The Kitchen in Wartime'

Some food from each group should be chosen each day

GROUP I	GROUP II
BODY-BUILDING FOODS	**ENERGY FOODS**
They build the body and prevent the tissues wearing out.	They provide fuel for the human body.
Milk	Potatoes
Cheese	Bread and Flour
Eggs	Oatmeal
Meat	Rice, Sago
Fish	Sugar
	Dried Fruit
Many vegetable foods such as peas and beans, bread and potatoes, help in body-building ; but they are not such good body-builders as these five.	Honey
	Cheese
	Butter or Margarine
	Dripping, Suet, Lard
	Bacon and Ham

GROUP III	GROUP IV
PROTECTIVE FOODS	
They protect us from disease.	
Milk	Potatoes
Butter or Margarine	Green Vegetables and Salads
Cheese	Fruit (fresh or canned, but not dried)
Eggs	Carrots
Herrings, Salmon (canned or fresh)	Tomatoes

Radio Times, August 9, 1940 Vol. 68 No. 880 Registered at the G.P.O. as a Newspaper

PRICE TWOPENCE

PROGRAMMES FOR
August 11 — 17

RADIO TIMES
JOURNAL OF THE BRITISH BROADCASTING CORPORATION
(INCORPORATING WORLD-RADIO)

'Bombers over Germany'

point of view of the five men in a bomber's crew will be told in a dramatic broadcast on Thursday. This picture shows the crew of a bomber about to set off on one of the R.A.F.'s nightly raids on military objectives in Germany. The story of an actual air raid from the

ALSO THIS WEEK **The Rev. Pat McCormick** in a broadcast service. **Ralph Richardson** in the last act of 'Johnson over Jordan'. **'Anything Goes'** Diana Ward playing her stage part. **The Fol-de-Rols** The famous concert party. **Binnie Hale** and **Michael Redgrave** starring in 'Theatreland'. **Flotsam and Jetsam** Chief gloom-chasers in a new series. **'Armies of Free Men'** Feature programme by Tom Wintringham.

RADIO ✻ TIMES
JOURNAL OF THE BRITISH BROADCASTING CORPORATION

The war years 1940

RADIO'S CONCENTRATION

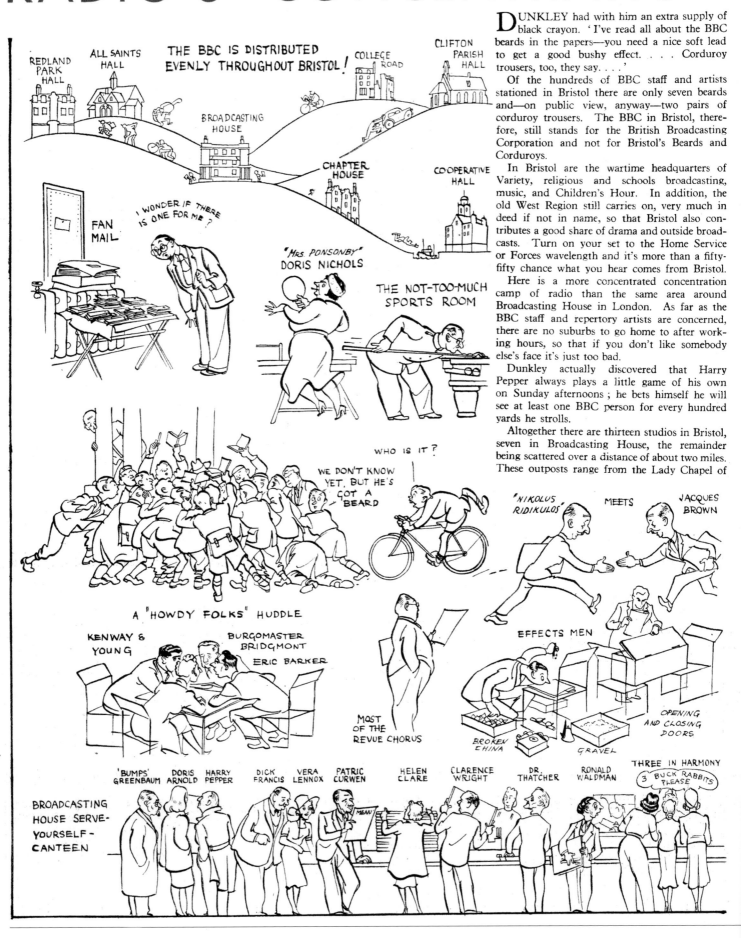

THE BBC IS DISTRIBUTED EVENLY THROUGHOUT BRISTOL!

REDLAND PARK HALL · ALL SAINTS HALL · BROADCASTING HOUSE · COLLEGE ROAD · CLIFTON PARISH HALL · CHAPTER HOUSE · CO-OPERATIVE HALL

FAN MAIL

I WONDER IF THERE IS ONE FOR ME?

"MRS. PONSONBY" DORIS NICHOLS

THE NOT-TOO-MUCH SPORTS ROOM

WHO IS IT?

WE DON'T KNOW YET, BUT HE'S GOT A BEARD

A "HOWDY FOLKS" HUDDLE

'NIKOLUS RIDIKULOS' MEETS JACQUES BROWN

EFFECTS MEN

OPENING AND CLOSING DOORS

BROKEN CHINA

GRAVEL

KENWAY & YOUNG · BURGOMASTER BRIDGMONT · ERIC BARKER

MOST OF THE REVUE CHORUS

THREE IN HARMONY

3 BUCK RABBITS PLEASE

BROADCASTING HOUSE SERVE-YOURSELF-CANTEEN

'BUMPS' GREENBAUM · DORIS ARNOLD · HARRY PEPPER · DICK FRANCIS · VERA LENNOX · PATRIC CURWEN · HELEN CLARE · CLARENCE WRIGHT · DR. THATCHER · RONALD WALDMAN

MENU

DUNKLEY had with him an extra supply of black crayon. 'I've read all about the BBC beards in the papers—you need a nice soft lead to get a good bushy effect. . . . Corduroy trousers, too, they say. . . .'

Of the hundreds of BBC staff and artists stationed in Bristol there are only seven beards and—on public view, anyway—two pairs of corduroy trousers. The BBC in Bristol, therefore, still stands for the British Broadcasting Corporation and not for Bristol's Beards and Corduroys.

In Bristol are the wartime headquarters of Variety, religious and schools broadcasting, music, and Children's Hour. In addition, the old West Region still carries on, very much in deed if not in name, so that Bristol also contributes a good share of drama and outside broadcasts. Turn on your set to the Home Service or Forces wavelength and it's more than a fifty-fifty chance what you hear comes from Bristol.

Here is a more concentrated concentration camp of radio than the same area around Broadcasting House in London. As far as the BBC staff and repertory artists are concerned, there are no suburbs to go home to after working hours, so that if you don't like somebody else's face it's just too bad.

Dunkley actually discovered that Harry Pepper always plays a little game of his own on Sunday afternoons ; he bets himself he will see at least one BBC person for every hundred yards he strolls.

Altogether there are thirteen studios in Bristol, seven in Broadcasting House, the remainder being scattered over a distance of about two miles. These outposts range from the Lady Chapel of

CAMP!

Jack Dunkley, popular RADIO TIMES artist, went to Bristol to see the radio stars back-stage. This is what he saw—

the Cathedral, where the morning services come from (just Studio 19 to the BBC), to a store-room in the Co-Operative Hall, where serious orchestral concerts come from, and three parish halls, Clifton, Redland Park, and All Saints'.

Clifton Parish Hall was converted at the outbreak of war into a fully-equipped studio within three days. There is undoubtedly a labyrinth of wires and plugs and switches and what-not beneath the floorboards, but to ordinary eyes there is little change. There still remains a stage, which seems haunted by the ghosts of innumerable amateur performances of *Charley's Aunt* and which is not used by the BBC (no, not even for 'Garrison Theatre'); leaded-glass windows framed in Gothic stonework; and two hundred or so chairs, battened together in rows, which come in useful for studio audiences.

There are microphones now, of course, gramophone turntables, and a glass-fronted control room that makes the engineers look like fish in an aquarium.

You can imagine how all this appealed to a simple soul like Dunkley, but his biggest thrill was to come later—when he learned that between broadcasts of dance music and other frivolities a Bible class still meets regularly at Redland Park Hall.

The frieze at the bottom of these two pages perhaps needs some explanation. It shows a typical scene in the new canteen at Bristol's Broadcasting House. You takes your choice on the left and pays your money at the cash desk on the right. There are as many as twenty-four tables in this restaurant, but the queue is so long at lunch-time that Dunkley would have wanted a specially wide edition of the RADIO TIMES to get it all in.

HAROLD RATHBONE

THE BBC IN BRISTOL
Bristol had become the wartime HQ for much of the BBC's output, including variety, religion, schools, music, drama and *Children's Hour*. In a May 1940 *RT*, the proliferation of BBC personnel was likened — rather unfortunately — to a concentration camp, and depicted by cartoonist Jack Dunkley. Notables included actor Jack Warner and a very early BBC watchdog, Barty.

Radio Times, August 30, 1940 Vol. 68 No. 883 Registered at the G.P.O. as a Newspaper

PRICE TWOPENCE

PROGRAMMES FOR
September 1 – 7

RADIO ✦ TIMES
JOURNAL OF THE BRITISH BROADCASTING CORPORATION
(INCORPORATING WORLD-RADIO)

'Napoleon Couldn't Do It'
More than a century ago Napoleon, master of Europe, planned to conquer Britain, but he failed. L. du Garde Peach draws a topical parallel in his play to be broadcast on Monday.

ALSO THIS WEEK:

'Calling All Workers!'
New Eric Coates march

Leslie Howard
A film star talks on film acting

The Minister of Information
Speaks to the children of the Empire

'Twelve Months Ago'
Story of the outbreak of war

Gibraltar
Dramatic chronicle of the Rock

Herbert Morrison
Says 'Keep At It!'

Jack Warner
'Garrison Theatre' from the stage

Jessie Matthews
In Saturday 'Music-Hall'

'Pig-Hoo-o-o-o-ey'
More P. G. Wodehouse

Radio Times, September 6, 1940 Vol. 68 No. 884 Registered at the G.P.O. as a Newspaper

PRICE TWOPENCE

PROGRAMMES FOR
September 8 – 14

RADIO ✦ TIMES
JOURNAL OF THE BRITISH BROADCASTING CORPORATION
(INCORPORATING WORLD-RADIO)

Cock-a-Doodle-Doo!

Charles B. Cochran (picture on right) presents the first of his all-star Saturday shows on September 14

ALSO THIS WEEK

National Day of Prayer
Special broadcasts on Sunday

Robert Donat
In Marlowe's 'Dr. Faustus'

'Gay Divorce'
Musical comedy with all-star cast

'Uniform House'
A famous theatre opens for the Forces

Arthur Askey
King Pin of Comedy

'Anchor Day'
London entertains the sailors

'France Fights On'
Story of the Free Frenchmen

BROADCASTS TO SCHOOLS 1940-41

Autumn Term, September 9 to December 13. Dates for Spring and Summer Terms will be announced later.

TIME a.m.	MONDAY	TUESDAY	WEDNESDAY	THURSDAY	FRIDAY	TIME a.m.
10.5	News Commentary Senior 11–15	News Commentary Senior 11–15	News Commentary Senior 11–15	News Commentary Senior 11–15	News Commentary	10.5
10.10						
11.0	Singing Together Junior and Senior 9–15	Physical Training (Halls) Junior 9–12	Music and Movement for Juniors Junior 7–9	Preparatory Concert Broadcasts		
11.20	Interval Music	Interval Music	Current Affairs Senior 11–15	Intermediate French 14 and over		
11.25	Senior English III Secondary and others 14-16	Games with Words Junior 9–12				
11.40	English for Under-Nines Junior 7–9	Talks for Fifth Forms	Broadcasts in Welsh	Senior Geography Senior 11–15		
12.0 p.m.	The Practice and Science of Gardening Senior 11–15	For Rural Schools Junior and Senior 9–15	Music Making Junior and Senior 9–15	Nature Study Junior 9–12		
1.50						
2.10	Interval Music	Interval Music	Interval Music	Interval Music		
2.15	World History Junior 9–12	For Under-Sevens	General Science Senior 12–15	Physical Training (Classrooms) Junior 9–12		
2.30		Interval Music		Interval Music		
2.35	Interval Music	Senior English II Senior 11–15	Interval Music	British History Senior 11–15		
2.40	Senior English I Senior 11–14		Junior English Junior 9–12			
3.0						

A copy of the detailed programme for the Autumn Term has been sent to every registered listening school. Any school already done so should write at once to the Secretary of the Central or Scottish Council for School Broadcasting, at Broadcasti

ONE YEAR ON...

In September 1940, a year after the war had started, *Radio Times* drew a "topical parallel" to Napoleon (above left) and heralded light-hearted variety from impresario Charles B Cochran (above right). School broadcasting was recognised as "a highly important national service" and *RT* printed a full schedule.

FOR SCHOOLS

'School broadcasting has come to be recognised as a highly important national service, the value of which increases as the general situation in the country becomes more difficult. To the teacher in particular it is of value in many ways.' So says the Board of Education in its recently-issued memorandum No. 22 on the use of school broadcasts in war-time, and it goes on to specify the ways in which these broadcasts can be of use to the teacher during the war. The memorandum also outlines the main features of the new programme for the autumn term. This term starts on September 9, and the full schedule of broadcasts will appear in next week's RADIO TIMES.

Radio Times, November 1, 1940   Vol. 69   No. 892   Registered at the G.P.O. as a Newspaper

PRICE TWOPENCE

PROGRAMMES FOR
November 3 — 9

RADIO ✸ TIMES

JOURNAL OF THE BRITISH BROADCASTING CORPORATION

(INCORPORATING WORLD-RADIO)

Fighter

Pilot

A feature programme showing you the fighter pilots of the R.A.F. in training will be broadcast on Tuesday. Here is a pilot, typical of the young men who fly the Spitfires and Hurricanes
(page 16)

FIGHTER PILOT
As the country suffered the onslaught of the Blitz, in November *Radio Times* celebrated the heroism of RAF fighter pilots. The 30-minute broadcast, written and produced by Cecil McGivern, followed a pilot through the RAF's intensive training programme until the moment he was ready to take to the skies in a Spitfire or Hurricane.

MINISTRY **M of F** OF FOOD

THE WEEK'S FOOD FACTS Nº 8

Do without that second helping, that extra snack, unless you really need them. Turn today's scraps into tomorrow's soups and savouries. *Our waste is Hitler's weapon.*

Save food! Save money! Save cargo space for munitions!

Remember to turn on the wireless at 8.15 every morning. You'll hear many useful household hints

ON THE KITCHEN FRONT

BLACKBERRY JAM

Allow 1 lb. sugar to each lb. fruit. The blackberries must not be over-ripe. Put the fruit in a pan, and after sprinkling the sugar over it, let it stand for 3 or 4 hours. Place the pan over a low fire and stir with a wooden spoon until the sugar is quite dissolved and the mixture comes to the boil. Boil rapidly for 15 minutes stirring all the time. Then begin to test by cooling a little jam on a plate. If the surface sets and wrinkles when you push it with your finger, the jam is at setting-point. Take the pan from the fire. Cool a little. Remove the scum if it is very thick and pour the jam into clean, dry, *warm* jars. Cover immediately. *If the jam is for immediate use, only ¾ lb. sugar is necessary for each lb. fruit.*

A Grand Use for Stale Bread

Cut the stale ends of your loaves into neat pieces and bake them in the oven whenever you happen to have it on. They make crisp, delicious rusks, excellent for the children's teeth.

Grated Carrot Sandwich

Carrots are an exceptionally health-giving food and are rich in natural sugar. A grated carrot sandwich, preferably made with wholemeal bread, is a fine sustainer for an energetic child.

HEALTH HINT.

Steam your vegetables rather than boil them. Steaming conserves their goodness. If you have to boil them, use very little water and save that water for gravy or soup. Never over-cook them. It wastes fuel and destroys much of their nourishing content.

THE MINISTRY OF FOOD LONDON, S.W.1

MINISTRY **M of F** OF FOOD

THE WEEK'S FOOD FACTS Nº 9

"An army marches on its stomach." In this war, where every kitchen is in the front line, we *all* march on our stomachs.

Today science offers to help us to victory on the kitchen front. Everyone knows that certain foods are needed for energy and for body-building. But do you realise that other foods (rich in vitamins and mineral salts) are essential for *protecting us from illness?* Below there is a list of these 'medicine' foods, which science calls the *protective* foods. Read on if you want to know what to eat for health.

ON THE KITCHEN FRONT

CHIEF PROTECTIVE FOODS	
Milk	Potatoes
Butter or Margarine	Green Vegetables (fresh or canned but not dried)
Cheese	Salads
Eggs	Fruit (fresh or canned but not dried)
Herrings (fresh, canned or salt)	
Salmon (fresh or canned)	Carrots
	Tomatoes
Liver	Wholemeal Bread

TWO WAYS OF PRESERVING TOMATOES.

Tomato Puree. Wash the tomatoes and cut in quarters; heat in a covered saucepan until they are quite soft. A quarter-ounce of salt and a quarter-ounce of sugar to each two pounds of tomatoes may be added if desired. Rub the pulp through a sieve. Return it to the pan and reheat. Pour immediately into clean *hot* jars and seal either with mutton fat, or with three or four rounds of thin paper brushed with home-made paste and pressed down firmly one on top of the other over the neck of

Skinned whole Tomatoes in Brine. Blanch the tomatoes in boiling water for about half-a-minute; then put in cold water. Peel the tomatoes and pack in screw-band or clip-top jars. Cover with brine made from half an ounce of salt to one quart of water. A very little sugar (about a quarter of an ounce) may be added to the brine if desired. Sterilise in the same way as for bottled fruit, but raise the temperature to 190° F. in 1½ hours and maintain this temperature for 30 minutes.

SWEDES AND TURNIPS EN CASSEROLE.

Don't always eat swedes and turnips with meat. Excellent food and make a course by themselves. [...] or turnips and [...] pieces. [...] in a ho[...] lid. [...]

THE MINISTRY OF [FOOD]

MINISTRY OF FOOD

THE WEEK'S FOOD FACTS № 13

WE help the war effort if we buy what happens to be plentiful in our own locality. Stocks naturally vary a little in different parts of the country, but here is a " plenty list " which applies to most places:

HOME-KILLED MEAT · COFFEE · POTATOES
OATMEAL · HOME-GROWN VEGETABLES

ON THE KITCHEN FRONT

How to Dry Apples

We may be short of apples later in the year—through bringing munitions instead of apples in the ships from Canada. So here is a way of preserving the present supply—it can be used for windfalls or blemished fruit. Wipe the apples, remove cores with a round corer and peel thinly. Cut out any blemishes. Slice into rings about ¼" thick. Steep the rings for 10 minutes in water containing 1½ ozs. salt to the gallon.

Thread the rings on sticks or spread on slatted trays or cake racks covered with muslin. Dry in a very cool oven (leaving the door open to let the steam escape) or over a hot cylinder or on the rack of a stove, until they resemble chamois leather. The temperature should not exceed 120° F. At this heat the process usually takes about 4 hours. Turn once or twice during drying. Cool for 12 hours, then pack in paper bags, jars or tins and store in a dry place.

How to Make Porridge

A double saucepan or porringer is excellent for making porridge. If you have not got one, use a 2 lb. stone jam jar in a saucepan of boiling water.

Allow 2 ozs. medium oatmeal to 1 pint water. Bring the water to the boil. Sprinkle in the oatmeal, stirring all the time. Sprinkle slowly so that the water does not go off the boil. Boil and stir for 5 minutes, then put in a level teaspoonful of salt. Cover the pan and simmer for about 45 minutes, stirring occasionally.

If you have a hay-box (see Food Facts No. 12 for how to make one) boil the porridge for 5 minutes as before, then leave in the hay-box all night. In the morning reheat and serve.

Two Ways with Swedes

BAKED

Swedes are delicious baked round the joint. Peel them thinly, cut into neat cubes and arrange round the meat in the baking tin. Baste from time to time. When they are golden brown they are ready.

MASHED

If preferred, boil the swedes in a very little salted water until tender. Drain (using the water for gravy) and mash with a little dripping. Add a dash of pepper and serve piping hot.

Home-Killed Meat

Buy home-killed meat—and so assist our farmers and help to build up our reserves of imported meat. This needn't increase your housekeeping bills. Home-killed second quality is as good as imported and just as cheap. For instance, home-killed second quality boneless silverside, which goes such a long way with carrots and dumplings, costs 1/4d per lb.

Beef cuts for stews are excellent bargains. Boneless neck of beef (1/2d per lb. first quality and 10d. second quality) is ideal pie and pudding meat. You can make rich soups from clod and sticking, or knee joints (get the butcher to crack the bones for you).

Other economical cuts are brisket of beef, breast of mutton, sheeps' hearts, hand with foot (pork), and knuckle of veal.

Turn on your wireless at 8.15 every morning to hear useful hints and recipes

THE MINISTRY OF FOOD, LONDON, S.W.I

MINISTRY OF FOOD

FOOD FACTS

ON THE POTATO FRONT

POTATOES are home grown: we can eat as many as we like without using one inch of cargo space. Potatoes are good for us: they give us energy and bodily warmth and are what scientists call "protective" foods—that is, they help us to ward off infections. And remember — potatoes shouldn't always mean *boiled* potatoes. There's no end to the delicious ways in which they can be served.

Can you Cook Potatoes?

Before you answer " Yes " just read quickly through these questions.

1. Do you always *scrub* your potatoes rather than peel them ? (Nearly one-fifth of the value of the potato is lost if it's peeled.)

2. Do you conserve the goodness of your potatoes by baking or steaming them whenever possible ? (If you haven't a steamer, a colander put over a pan of boiling water and covered with the pan lid will do.)

3. When boiling potatoes, do you boil them only for 10-15 minutes, then drain, cover with a cloth and the lid and then let them cook in their own steam for about 20 minutes, to keep them whole and floury ?

4. Do you keep your baked potatoes nice and floury by bursting them gently when they are done, and returning them to the oven for a minute to let the steam escape ?

Potato Salad

The golden rule about Potato Salad is " Mix warm and eat cold."

Steam some potatoes in their skins, peel and cut them into small chunks while still warm, add a finely chopped raw onion and whatever kind of salad dressing you like best. Mix these together thoroughly with a wooden spoon. When the salad is cold, add a good sprinkling of chopped parsley.

Stuffed Baked Potatoes

Large baked potatoes can be stuffed in a great variety of ways. Here are three suggestions:

1. Cut the potato in half lengthwise, scoop out most of the inside and mix in a basin with pepper and salt and about 2 ozs. of grated cheese. Pile the mixture into the potato cases, sprinkle the tops with a little more grated cheese and return to the oven to brown.

2. Mix the scooped-out potato with about 4 ozs. of cooked meat or fish, finely chopped. Season with salt and pepper, pile into the cases, sprinkle with chopped parsley and reheat in the oven.

3. Mix the scooped-out potato with any left-over cooked vegetables and serve as above.

Potato Pastry

There's no end to the things you can make out of potato. Try this recipe some time. You'll need :—

4 ozs. sieved, cooked potatoes, ½ teaspoonful salt, 8 ozs. plain flour, 3 ozs. cooking fat, 2 teaspoonfuls baking powder.

Sieve the flour with the baking powder and salt. Rub the fat into the flour, add the potato and rub in lightly. Mix to a very dry dough with a small quantity of cold water. Knead well with the fingers and roll out. This is delicious with either sweet or savoury dishes.

Cautionary Tale !

Those who have the will to win
Cook potatoes in their skin,
Knowing that the sight of peelings
Deeply hurts Lord Woolton's feelings.

Remember to turn on the wireless at 8.15 every morning to hear useful hints and recipes.

THE MINISTRY OF FOOD LONDON S.W.I

RADIO TIMES
JOURNAL OF THE BRITISH BROADCASTING CORPORATION
The war years 1940

ERIC FRASER

Born in 1902 and graduating from Goldsmiths in 1924, Eric Fraser had been drawing for *Radio Times* since 1926. Known for his distinctive stark style, he produced illustrations for *RT* covers, articles and listings throughout the war. When later asked about working to *RT's* tight deadlines, he replied, "I think the challenge of having to produce a drawing in such a short time, worrying as it was, did produce an ability to draw upon hidden reserves of energy, which are not normally used... I suppose we all have these hidden reserves, which are there to call upon in an emergency, and, as far as I was concerned, every commission I received from *Radio Times* was an emergency." Fraser was still contributing to *RT* shortly before his death in 1983.

Five short plays by Berthold Brecht will be broadcast tonight at 9.40 depicting typical incidents in the lives of the ordinary German man and woman under the rule of the Nazis.

48

fraser

...chines ! That was all I saw in the ranks of the German army. Flying ...chines, crawling machines, talking machines, killing machines ! Machines ! Machines !

This play by G. R. Rainier, which illustrates how careless talk, however innocent it may seem at the time, might be pieced together by the enemy and give away a vital secret, will be broadcast again tonight at 10.0.

Radio Times, December 20, 1940   Vol. 69   No. 899   Registered at the G.P.O. as a Newspaper

PRICE TWOPENCE

PROGRAMMES FOR
December 22 — 28

RADIO ✳ TIMES

JOURNAL OF THE BRITISH BROADCASTING CORPORATION

{INCORPORATING WORLD-RADIO}

Here is the Christmas News and this is Father Christmas reading it....

'Christmas Under Fire'

Radio tour of the Empire in the front line (page 20)

'From Across the Atlantic'

Broadcasts from Canada (page 13), dance band exchange (page 21), and Hollywood greetings (page 23)

Evacuee Children

Sending greetings to their parents in three programmes (pages 20 and 23)

Pantomimes

Tour of three Northern pantos (page 16), 'The Forty Thieves' and 'The Sleeping Beauty' (page 22), 'Aladdin' (page 26)

Stars of the Week

Edith Evans, John Gielgud, and Peggy Ashcroft (page 11), Eva Turner (page 12), John McCormack, Arthur Askey, Richard Murdoch, Elsie and Doris Waters, and Jack Warner (page 21), Sir Harry Lauder (page 30)

Music

Handel's 'Messiah' (page 11)

CHRISTMAS 1940

Artist John Gilroy is perhaps best known for his "Guinness is good for you" poster campaign of the 1920s, but he was also a regular contributor to *Radio Times* and in 1940 he produced this hearty Father Christmas. To lend further festive cheer to the country, *RT* called upon its roster of popular artists (opposite page) – the most renowned being Heath Robinson, who came up with "Christmas Crime – the radio thief".

'Smile please!'

Seven popular artists give RADIO TIMES *readers a laugh this Christmas*

'He says it will be sixpence for charging the accumulator, and another five shillings for bringing it out here'

'Oi! Steady on—there's a bomb inside it!'

'Can you hear me, mother?'

Christmas Crime—the radio thief

'Since the News began the following communiqué has been received from the Air Ministry . . .'

'. . . Postman's knock—will someone just go outside . . .'

''Fraid this means we won't be home for the six o'clock News!'

RADIO ✴ TIMES
JOURNAL OF THE BRITISH BROADCASTING CORPORATION

The war years 1941

1941

COMMUNITY

WHISTLING

Join in and whistle with Ronald Gourley and the boys this evening at 6.30

GIVE IT'EM HOT

Radio Times, January 3, 1941 Vol. 70 No. 901 Registered at the G.P.O. as a Newspaper

PROGRAMMES FOR
January 5 — 11

PRICE TWOPENCE

RADIO ✠ TIMES
JOURNAL OF THE BRITISH BROADCASTING CORPORATION
(INCORPORATING WORLD-RADIO)

EMLYN WILLIAMS

will include scenes from his notable plays 'The Corn is Green', 'Night Must Fall', and 'The Light of Heart' in his broadcast this week in the Sunday series 'The BBC Presents'

(Page 8)

ALSO ——————

JOHN McCORMACK
Singing Tom Moore's songs (page 8)

ALICE DELYSIA
Radio version of 'Mother of Pearl' (page 11)

HARDY'S WESSEX
Feature programme (page 11)

GEORGE WASHINGTON
'These Men Were Free' (page 14)

JESSIE MATTHEWS
        and SONNIE HALE
In a stage broadcast of 'Aladdin' (page 20)

ALBERT CHEVALIER
'Good Old Timer' (page 22)

'MADAM BUTTERFLY'
With the Sadler's Wells Company (page 23)

VIC OLIVER
        and SARAH CHURCHILL
In Saturday 'Star-Time' (page 26)

In the face of adversity

As war spread around the world, the British public inured itself to rationing, blackouts and the Blitz. The BBC provided information and diversions – all covered by *Radio Times...*

The Duchess and the Wrens

A new Royal recruit to the microphone

HERE is good news for listeners. On Monday, H.R.H. the Duchess of Kent, who has never before broadcast from a studio—who, in fact, has never been heard on the air since a short time after her marriage in 1934—is to give a talk on that famous Service, the Women's Royal Naval Service, better known, perhaps, as the W.R.N.S. or Wrens.

As Commandant of the Wrens, Her Royal Highness has seen more than a little of their work, for she has inspected them at many naval ports. She has seen them formally on parade ; she has seen them at work and at play ; she has seen recruits in training at the Royal Naval College, Greenwich ; and skilled workers at their jobs in the Naval Shore Establishments, where each of them, in doing that job, is releasing a man to join the Fleet. It is therefore not as an outsider that she will speak, but as a member of the Service, who thoroughly understands its working conditions.

Her Royal Highness is no mere figurehead in the Wrens, but an active and inspiring Commandant. Her inspections have been carried out under all conditions and in all weathers. This resolute keeping of her engagements gives the greatest pleasure and encouragement to the members of the Service.

The great personal interest taken by the Duchess in the W.R.N.S. has never been more clearly seen than when she visited a station in Scotland a few weeks ago. After inspecting the Wrens on parade, she went to the men's quarters, where the Wrens look after the feeding arrangements, then to the living-quarters of the Wrens themselves, where she was shown all details of the domestic affairs and the plans made for their comfort. Then she went to the canteen, where Wrens were having ' elevenses ', and finally was shown the various offices of the whole Naval Establishment, where Wrens were working under Naval officers as coders, clerks, secretaries, telephone operators, etc. ; And many indeed *are* still required—as telephonists, typists, wireless operators, cooks, and so on.

Since, then, the Duchess knows so much about the Service from the inside, she is clearly well qualified to speak about the work it is doing for the country at war ; and listeners may expect to hear a vivid and interesting talk from her on Monday.

Radio Times, January 17, 1941 Vol. 70 No. 903 Registered at the G.P.O. as a Newspaper

PRICE TWOPENCE

RADIO ✶ TIMES
JOURNAL OF THE BRITISH BROADCASTING CORPORATION
(INCORPORATING WORLD-RADIO)

PROGRAMMES FOR
January 19 – 25

THE DUCHESS OF KENT

On Monday Her Royal Highness will broadcast as Commandant of the Women's Royal Naval Service. This will be her first studio broadcast. (Page 11 and article, page 4)

ALSO

ROYALTY AND WRENS

In January 1941, *Radio Times* hailed the Duchess of Kent as an "active and inspiring Commandant" of the Women's Royal Naval Service, aka the Wrens.

OPPOSITE PAGE reporter Robin Duff reflected on the onset of the Blitz the previous year. J Tudor Jones spelt out how transmissions were reaching overseas: "People in fallen France are humming defiant tunes and murmuring defiant slogans which they have learnt from the BBC."

'The BBC European Services give to all oppressed people *their songs*'

OBSERVING THE 'BLITZ'
By Robin Duff

'... recorded by our observer, Robin Duff'—you have heard the phrase often enough in the News. Here is his own story.

IT all started at Dover. I had been an announcer, but had always wanted work like this. The chance came soon after Charles Gardner's famous air-battle commentary, when I was sent down to get some more sounds of planes. We got them all right ; and 'they' nearly got us. We were watching our (as we thought) Hurricanes, when one of them swerved to attack a balloon, missed it, and decided to take us as second best. We got down pretty quickly, and I just remembered to hold the mike above my head—or whatever bit of me was uppermost just then ! When we played the record later, the machine-gun bullets sounded unpleasantly close.

'We' were Arthur Phillips, Leonard Lewis, and myself. The other two look after the technical side. They don't get much limelight, and you don't often hear their names. But wherever we want to record, there they go—any place, any time. I, for one, have a good deal to thank them for.

Bursting Shells

A few days later I did a commentary on the first shelling of a convoy in the Straits. It wasn't very easy to keep my voice quite steady, as some of the shells were bursting pretty close in front of us a dead line. We sent the records up to London by train, and listened to them in the nine o'clock News. We were in a restaurant, and as the last crash came on the radio all the plates rattled, and the whole room shook. The first shell of the night bombardment had arrived at Dover. This time we heard the screech, as they flew overhead ; and sometimes, from the top of the cliff, we could see them explode. We ended the night with me reading a description by the light of the headlamps, at two o'clock. The record was meant to catch the train at four. It didn't ; but that's another story.

Then came the 'blitz'. On the first day I was at the oil fire at Thames-side, and since then I've spent a good many nights at fires. I've made some very good friends there, and learnt a certain amount about the job.

No Commentary

I remember one night especially —the night the barrage started. I was at a big fire with Skipper Arnell and Phil, meaning to record a commentary. But we soon threw off our coats and got down to fighting the fire. That night produced one of the best sights I ever hope to see. We found that Skipper was missing, and ran him to earth on a roof. With gas-mask on, he was wildly flinging bales of paper and boxes of pencils from a window. They burnt merrily in the air. Phil wasn't to be outdone. He rushed into the building, and staggered out with a desk. Over the parapet it went, brilliantly salvaged. What it was like when it reached the ground is beside the point. A few minutes later the roof fell in.

Since that night I've been around the streets during the raids, to give a picture to America of what it was really like. I've been out with the Rescue and Demolition squads on their dangerous and sickening work, and I've learnt to admire these men more than most. There have been nights in the big public shelters, talking to the shelter-marshals about some of the problems they have to cope with ; more fires ; visits to some of the children who were torpedoed on their way to Canada ; a journey to the top of one of the Fire Brigade's turn-table ladders.

We Keep Moving

I have become quite familiar with gutters in most parts of London, and have learned to move with incredible speed. Moving, as a matter of fact, has been one of the main problems, and on the whole the pillion seat of a despatch-rider's motor-bike has been the most successful.

Then there was a night at a bomber station while we were raiding Germany ; and an afternoon with the Fighter Command. Sometimes the job takes us over to Ireland, and often to Scotland. Wherever the job, it's always interesting.

Robin Duff (left) gathering his material on the spot from A.R.P. workers after a London raid

Slogans for Free Europe
How the BBC broadcasts lead the laugh against Nazis and Fascists

By J. TUDOR JONES, of the BBC's European Department

PEOPLE in fallen France are humming defiant tunes and murmuring defiant slogans which they have learnt from the BBC.

The young Frenchman who had 'had enough of the Boche' and flew to England in his 'taxi' the other week told us how the BBC's Taranto verses had caught on. Barely twelve hours after the story of the Naval Air Arm's dashing attack became known, France (and others) were listening to a merry parody from London of a poem by Chénier:

Elle a vécu, Musso, la flotte Tarentine
(It's a goner, Musso, the Tarentinian fleet)

The airman also said that a garage hand who attended to his car in Brittany hummed 'Radio Paris Ment' (Radio Paris Lies), one of the slogan-songs of the French section of the BBC European Department.

This is but a glimpse of the unceasing mental warfare that goes on. The enemy is attacked in his own country, the peoples under his domination are given hope and encouragement, and everything that can be done to make his armies downcast is done.

News is Not All

Straight and serious talks, of course, go out in plenty, all based on the latest intelligence and all carefully aimed. News forms the backbone of the broadcasts, but European man needs more ; those from whom leaders are likely to arise want something to help them to remain human while the war takes its course. The programme sections see to that. Moreover, they press home the news themes by treating them in a different way. Frenchmen may forget how many ships were sunk at Taranto, but they will remember how they laughed when they heard 'La Flotte Tarentine'. They cannot quote the lies of Radio Paris, but they all sing 'Radio Paris Ment' and believe it.

It is a German idea, really, turned against its authors. The slogans of Ferdonnet (the French Haw-Haw) about England fighting to the last Frenchman, and the like, did a lot to prepare the French collapse. The Germans, realising the failure of their recent propaganda in France, have even been trying slogans again. Our slogans, however, will have the advantage, for they will be applied to concrete, verifiable facts, such as German infiltration and pillage, and to almost universal grievances, such as Alsace-Lorraine and food shortage.

There are also 'characters' who speak to Europe on BBC wave-

A Nazi journal pays British broadcasting the compliment of printing this satirical cartoon as a warning to 'misguided' Germans who listen to London .

lengths. A woman, 'Frau Wernicke', who might be called a Berlin Cockney, hides her anti-Nazi politics under a cloak of injured innocence and damns the people she is talking to (the Blockwart, the Nazi neighbour, or the air-raid warden) with their own arguments.

'Svejk', in the Czech programme, is the 'stupid' man-in-the-street hero of a novel that appeared after the last war, and is now the symbol of resistance disguised as stupidity. In the Flemish programme of Radio Belgique there appears 'Jan Moedwil', a common type of Fleming, full of good humour, who insists on those small things in Flemish life to which the Flemings were most attached and which the Germans are suppressing.

The Germans have banned the singing of popular songs in Denmark, 'as it does not fit in with the present serious times'. The BBC European Services give to all oppressed people their songs.

Goebbels Doesn't Like It

No longer can Dr. Goebbels say that our propaganda is a 'sitting bird'. There is evidence, indeed, that the enemy is coming to regard our broadcasts as a menace. The German paper *Die Woche* recently warned its readers that British lies were becoming more systematic and that the standard of announcing had recently improved. Some favourite BBC themes were analysed to show how the system was worked. This article was very much on a par with the explanatory talks on Haw-Haw given in the BBC Home Service last year. This is all very gratifying and cheering to our news and programme staffs, who know that the work they are doing is part of the war effort and is but a beginning.

RADIO TIMES

JOURNAL OF THE BRITISH BROADCASTING CORPORATION

The war years 1941

What you can do in the *RAF*

Flying Duties. The R.A.F. wants keen, fit men between the ages of 17¼-32 to volunteer for flying duties. Even if you have registered, you can still volunteer. Maximum ages— for pilots 30, for air observers or wireless operator/air gunners 32.

If you need coaching to the standard of education required for flying duties, are aged 17¼-31, and are in other respects suitable, tuition will be provided for you near your own home, at the expense of the Air Ministry. Service training does not begin until 18.

Flight Mechanics. Skilled and semi-skilled tradesmen are needed to maintain and repair air frames, engines, armament and equipment. There are also vacancies for unreserved men who are mechanically minded, handy with tools and willing to be trained.

A.T.C. Those who are between 16-18 and, therefore, still too young for flying duties, should enrol in the Air Training Corps. Having thus obtained valuable preliminary experience they will be able to enrol in the R.A.F. at 17¼. Squadrons are being formed in schools, universities and in chief towns.

W.A.A.F. The W.A.A.F. wants women keen to help in the great work of the flying men of the R.A.F. If you have had experience as a Secretary, Typist, Shop Assistant, or Cook, you can be readily trained for important duties.

For fuller information about any of the above duties, apply to the R.A.F. Section of your nearest Combined Recruiting Centre (address from any Employment Exchange). If you cannot call, write today for details.

To Air Ministry Information Bureau, Kingsway London, W.C.2. *Please send me latest details o*

Flying Duties ☐

Free tuition scheme ☐ *NAME*...........................

Flight Mechanics ☐ *ADDRESS*

A.T.C. ☐

W.A.A.F. ☐

X against the one in **which you are** interested. RT/28/3

EVERY NEW PLANE

NEEDS A PILOT

And this is where you come in, you wh are 17¼ and not yet 33. Your country ha a job for you—a job that calls for fitness dash, initiative, intelligence, responsibility A young man's job— a war-winning job. We're getting the planes—we must get the men !

If you are 17¼ and not yet 33, go to the R.A.F. Section of the nearest Combined Recruiting Centre (address from any Employment E change) and say you wish to volunteer for Flying Duties. Ce reserved men can now volunteer for Pilot and Observer duties. aged 17¼ but not yet 31 who are suitable for flying duties Observer, but require tuition to pass the educational te coached in their spare time, free of cost.

Fly with the **RAF**

ADDRESS

RT/16/5

No woman
will ever have peace in her heart until she helps this man !

Would you hesitate ? . . . If you knew you could actively help to harass and confuse and frustrate the evil forces that threaten his life and yours . . . would you hesitate ? You know you wouldn't. And you *can* help to cripple the enemy now, by joining the A.T.S. You *can* do something vital and essential. Do not let anyone hold you back.

Write for the full story of the A.T.S and all the opportunities it offers you, to the AUXILIARY TERRITORIAL SERVICE, A.G.18/ P b, Hobart House, Grosvenor Gardens, London, S.W.1 (on a p.c. please). Or call and have a friendly talk at an Employment Exchange or any A.T.S or Army recruiting centre.

Because he needs help urgently join the A.T.S

'My job is Radiolocation'

"I can't tell you JUST what I'm doing"

"Radiolocation—one of the best kept secrets of the war. It helped to win the Battle of Britain and it's going to win more battles for the Royal Air Force. It's thrilling work . . . and you've got to be quick in the uptake to do it. The Radiolocator sends out electric waves that patrol the air. The waves radio messages back to me. Every single thing is recorded. My eyes must be on the look-out all the time to receive the incoming signals. I can't tell you about *them*, of course. They're secret and confidential."

Radiolocation is a brand new science. It has enormous possibilities now in war. It will have a great future in the post war world when trained operators will be invaluable. Radiolocation may well be the "discovery of the century." Hundreds of women are needed immediately by the W.A.A.F. for Radiolocation work. They must be mentally alert and accurate. First-class eyesight and sound nerves are essential. Women who are able to take responsibility under active service conditions and can pick up a new idea quickly, have a magnificent chance to pioneer in a great new scientific discovery. An exceptional education is not required, but women who can offer qualifications in physics increase their chances of promotion to commissioned rank.

● *Age limits 17½ to 35. Go to the R.A.F. section of the nearest Combined Recruiting Centre or W.A.A.F. Sub-Recruiting Depot, and say you have come to enrol as a Radio Operator on Radiolocation duties in the W.A.A.F., or else post the coupon below.*

Learn Radiolocation in the

To Air Ministry Information Bureau, Adastral House, Kingsway, W.C.2.
Please send me full details of service with the W.A.A.F. as Radio Operator.

NAME ....

ADDRESS

RT 11/7

Radio Times, May 9, 1941 Vol. 71 No. 919 Registered at the G.P.O. as a Newspaper

PRICE TWOPENCE

MR. CHURCHILL'S BROADCAST
IN FULL (pages 8 to 10)

RADIO TIMES

JOURNAL OF THE BRITISH BROADCASTING CORPORATION

(INCORPORATING WORLD-RADIO)

TANK CREWS
IN TRAINING

On Saturday the microphone will take you to a Tank School to hear something of the training of the crews (page 36)

ALSO THIS WEEK

The Minister of Information. Mr. Duff Cooper will give the Sunday night Postscript this week (p. 12)

Christian Foundations. Public speeches by the Archbishop of Canterbury and Cardinal Hinsley (p. 13)

PLAYS
'The Torch' by G. Rodney Rainier (p. 17)
'The Door of Opportunity' by Somerset Maugham (p. 20)
'The High Road' by Frederick Lonsdale (p. 25)
'Post Mortem' by Malcolm Graeme (p. 26)
'Twenty Years a-Growing' by Maurice O'Sullivan (p. 28)

VARIETY
Arthur Askey and Richard Murdoch, Graham Moffatt and Moore Marriott; Jessie Matthews and Sonnie Hale (p. 12)
Archie de Bear, Alice Delysia (p. 15)
Beatrice Lillie in three shows (pp. 19, 23, and 26)
Return of Saturday 'Music-Hall' (p. 36)

MUSICAL SHOWS: 'Shephard's Pie', another broadcast (p. 18); 'The Command Performance', radio version (p. 33)

CHURCHILL'S SPEECH

Winston Churchill became prime minister in May 1940. On 27 April 1941, he gave a rousing speech that painted a vivid picture of the national mood: "I have seen many painful scenes of havoc, and of fine buildings, and acres of cottage homes, blasted into rubble heaps of ruin. But it is just in those very places where the malice of the savage enemy has done its worst, and where the ordeal of the men, women, and children has been most severe, that I found their morale most high and splendid."

Radio Times printed his speech in full two weeks later and it is reproduced across the following pages...

'The **British nation** is stirred and moved as it had never been at any time in its **long, eventful, famous** history ,

RADIO ✶ TIMES
JOURNAL OF THE BRITISH BROADCASTING CORPORATION
The war years 1941

MR. CHURCHILL'S BROADCAST IN FULL

'The cause of freedom

I WAS asked last week whether I was aware of some uneasiness which it was said existed in the country on account of the gravity, as it was described, of the war situation. So I thought it would be a good thing to go and see for myself what this 'uneasiness' amounted to, and I went to some of our great cities and seaports which have been most heavily bombed, and to some of the places where the poorest people have got it worst. I have come back not only reassured but refreshed. To leave the offices in Whitehall, with their ceaseless hum of activity and stress, and to go out to the 'Front', by which I mean the streets and wharves of London or Liverpool, Manchester, Cardiff, Swansea, or Bristol, is like going out of a hothouse on to the bridge of a fighting ship. It is a tonic which I should recommend any who are suffering from fretfulness to take in strong doses when they have need of it.

It is quite true that I have seen many painful scenes of havoc, and of fine buildings, and acres of cottage homes, blasted into rubble heaps of ruin. But it is just in those very places where the malice of the savage enemy has done its worst, and where the ordeal of the men, women, and children has been most severe, that I found their morale most high and splendid. Indeed, I felt encompassed by an exaltation of spirit in the people which seemed to lift mankind and its troubles above the level of material facts, into that joyous serenity we think belongs to a better world than this.

The nation is stirred

Of their kindness to me I cannot speak, because I have never sought it or dreamed of it, and can never deserve it. I can only assure you that I and my colleagues—or comrades, rather, for that is what they are—will toil with every scrap of life and strength according to the lights that are granted to us, not to fail these people, or be wholly unworthy of their faithful and generous regard.

The British nation is stirred and moved as it had never been at any time in its long, eventful, famous history, and it is no hackneyed trope of speech to say that they mean to conquer or to die.

What a triumph the life of these battered cities is, over the worst that fire and bomb can do ! What a vindication of the civilised and decent way of living we have been trying to work for and

work towards in our island ! What a proof of the virtues of free institutions ! What a test of the quality of our local authorities—and of institutions and customs and societies so steadily built ! This ordeal by fire has even, in a certain sense, exhilarated the manhood and the womanhood of Britain. The sublime but also terrible and sombre experiences and emotions of the battlefield which for centuries had been reserved for the soldiers and sailors, are now shared for good or ill by the entire population. All are proud to be under the fire of the enemy. Old men, little children, the crippled veterans of former wars ; aged women, the ordinary hard-pressed citizen or subject of the King (as he likes to call himself) ; the sturdy workmen who swing the hammers or load the ships ; skilful craftsmen ; the members of every kind of A.R.P. service—are proud to feel that they stand in the line together with our fighting men, when one of the greatest of causes is being fought out—as fought out it will be, to the end. This is indeed the grand heroic period of our history—and the light of glory shines on all.

You may imagine how deeply I feel my own responsibility to all these people ; my responsibility to bear my part in bringing them safely out of this long, stern, scowling valley through which we are marching, and not to demand from them their sacrifices and exertions in vain.

A call which we could not resist

I have thought in this difficult period when so much fighting and so many critical and complicated manœuvres are going on, that it is above all things important that our policy and conduct should be upon the highest level, and that honour should be our guide. Very few people realise how small were the forces with which General Wavell (that fine commander whom we cheered in good days and will back through bad)—how small were the forces which took the bulk of the Italian masses in Libya prisoners. In none of his successive victories could General Wavell maintain in the desert or bring into action more than two Divisions or about 30,000 men. When we reached Benghazi, and what was left of Mussolini's legions scurried back along the dusty road to Tripoli, a call was made upon us which we could not

resist. Let me tell you about that call.

You will remember how in November the Italian Dictator fell upon the unoffending Greeks, and without reason and without warning invaded their country ; and how the Greek nation, reviving their classic fame, hurled his armies back at the double-quick. Meanwhile, Hitler, who had been creeping and worming his way steadily forward, doping and poisoning and pinioning, one after the other, Hungary, Rumania, and Bulgaria —suddenly made it clear that he would come to the rescue of his fellow criminal. The lack of unity among the Balkan States had enabled him to build up a mighty army in their midst. While nearly all the Greek troops were busy beating the Italians, a tremendous German military machine suddenly towered up on their other frontier. In their mortal peril the Greeks turned to us for succour. Strained as were our own resources, we could not say them nay. By solemn guarantee given before the war, Great Britain had promised them her help. They declared they would fight for their native soil even if neither of their neighbours made common cause with them, and even if we left them to their fate. But we could not do that. There are rules against that kind of thing ; and to break those rules would be fatal to the honour of the British Empire, without which we could neither hope nor deserve to win this hard war. Military defeat or miscalculation can be redeemed. The fortunes of war are fickle and changing. But an act of shame would deprive us of the respect which we now enjoy throughout the world, and this would sap the vitals of our strength.

The sentiment of the United States

During the last year we have gained by our bearing and conduct a potent hold upon the sentiments of the people of the United States. Never, never in our history have we been held in such admiration and regard across the Atlantic Ocean. In that great Republic, now in much travail and stress of soul, it is customary to use all the many valid solid arguments about 'American interests' and 'American safety' which depend upon the destruction of Hitler and his foul gang and even fouler doctrines. But in the long run— believe me, for I know—the action of the United States will be dictated, not by methodical calcula-

tions of profit and loss, but by moral sentiment and by that gleaming flash of resolve which lifts the hearts of men and nations and springs from the spiritual foundations of human life itself.

We, for our part, were of course bound to hearken to the Greek appeal to the utmost limit of our strength. We put the case to the Dominions of Australia and New Zealand, and their Governments, without in any way ignoring the hazards, told us that they felt the same as we did.

Fulfilling our pledge to Greece

So an important part of the mobile portion of the Army of the Nile was sent to Greece in fulfilment of our pledge. It happened that the Divisions available and best suited to this task were from New Zealand and Australia, and that only about half the troops who took part in this dangerous expedition came from the Mother Country. I see the German propaganda is trying to make bad blood between us and Australia, by making out that we have used them to do what we would not have asked of the British Army. I shall leave it to Australia to deal with that taunt.

Let us see what has happened. We knew, of course, that the forces we could send to Greece would not by themselves alone be sufficient to stem the German tide of invasion. But there was a very real hope that the neighbours of Greece would by our intervention be drawn to stand in the line together with her while time remained. How nearly that came off will be known some day. The tragedy of Yugoslavia has been that these brave people had a Government who hoped to purchase an ignoble immunity by submission to the Nazi will. Thus when at last the people of Yugoslavia found out where they were being taken, and rose in one spontaneous surge of revolt, they saved the soul and future of their country : but it was already too late to save its territory. They had no time to mobilise their armies. They were struck down by the ruthless and highly mechanised Hun before they could even bring their armies into the field. Great disasters have occurred in the Balkans. Yugoslavia has been beaten down. Only in the mountains can she continue her resistance. The Greeks have been overwhelmed. Their victorious Albanian Army has been cut off and forced to surrender, and it has been left to the Anzacs

shall not be trampled down'

and their British comrades to fight their way back to the sea, leaving their mark on all who hindered them.

The whipped jackal

I turn aside from the stony path we have to tread, to indulge a moment of lighter relief. I daresay you have read in the newspapers that by a special proclamation the Italian dictator has congratulated the Italian army in Albania on the glorious laurels they have gained by their victory over the Greeks. Here, surely, is the world's record in the domain of the ridiculous and the contemptible! This whipped jackal, Mussolini, who to save his own skin has made all Italy a vassal state of Hitler's empire, comes frisking up at the side of the German tiger with yelpings not only of appetite—that can be understood—but even of triumph. Different things strike different people in different ways; but I am sure there are a great many millions in the British Empire and

in the United States, who will find a new object in life in making sure that when we come to the final reckoning, this absurd impostor shall be abandoned to public justice and universal scorn.

While these grievous events were taking place in the Balkan Peninsula and in Greece, our forces in Libya have sustained a vexatious and damaging defeat. The Germans advanced sooner and in greater strength than we or our Generals expected. The bulk of our armoured troops, which had played such a decisive part in beating the Italians, had to be re-fitted, and the single armoured brigade, which had been judged sufficient to hold the frontier till about the middle of May, was worsted and its vehicles largely destroyed by a somewhat stronger German armoured force. Our infantry, which had not exceeded one division, had to fall back upon the very large Imperial armies that have been assembled and can be nourished and maintained in the fertile delta of the Nile.

Tobruk—the fortress of Tobruk —which flanks any German advance on Egypt — we hold strongly. There we have repulsed many attacks, causing the enemy heavy losses and taking many prisoners. That is how the matter stands in Egypt and on the Libyan Front.

A harder task

We must now expect the war in the Mediterranean, on the sea, in the desert, and above all in the air, to become very fierce, varied, and widespread. We had cleaned the Italians out of Cyrenaica, and it now lies with us to purge that province of the Germans. That will be a harder task, and we cannot expect to do it at once. You know I never try to make out that defeats are victories. I have never underrated the German as a warrior. Indeed, I told you a month ago that the swift, unbroken course of victories which we had gained over the Italians could not possibly continue, and that misfortunes must

be expected. There is only one thing certain about war: that it is full of disappointments and also full of mistakes. It remains to be seen, however, whether it is the Germans who have made the mistake in trampling down the Balkan States and in making a river of blood and hate between themselves and the Greek and Yugoslav peoples. It remains also to be seen whether they have made a mistake in their attempt to invade Egypt with the forces and means of supply which they have now got. Taught by experience, I make it a rule not to prophesy about battles which have yet to be fought out. This, however, I will venture to say: that I should be very sorry to see the tasks of the combatants in the Middle East exchanged, and for General Wavell's armies to be in the position of the German invaders.

That is only a personal opinion, and I can well understand you may take a different view. It is certain that fresh dangers besides those

[continued overleaf

'So I thought it would be a good thing to go and see for myself...'

THE PRIME MINISTER'S BROADCAST CONTINUED

which threaten Egypt may come upon us in the Mediterranean. The war may spread to Spain and Morocco. It may spread eastward to Turkey and Russia. The Huns may lay their hands for a time upon the granaries of the Ukraine and the oil wells of the Caucasus. They may dominate the Black Sea. They may dominate the Caspian. Who can tell ? We shall do our best to meet them and fight them wherever they go. But there is one thing which is certain. There is one thing which rises out of the vast welter which is sure and solid and which no one in his senses can mistake. Hitler cannot find safety from avenging justice in the East, in the Middle East, or in the Far East. In order to win this war he must either conquer this island by invasion, or he must cut the ocean life-line which joins us to the United States.

The position at home

Let us look into these alternatives, if you will bear with me for a few minutes longer. When I spoke to you last, early in February, many people believed the Nazi boastings that the invasion of Britain was about to begin. It has not begun yet, and with every week that passes we grow stronger on the sea, in the air, and in the numbers, quality, training and equipment of the great armies that now guard our island. When I compare the position at home as it is today with what it was in the summer of last year, even after making allowance for a much more elaborate mechanical preparation on the part of the enemy, I feel that we have very much to be thankful for, and I believe that provided our exertions and our vigilance are not relaxed even for a moment, we may be confident that we shall give a very good account of ourselves. More than that it would be boastful to say. Less than that it would be foolish to believe.

Atlantic life-line

But how about our life-line across the Atlantic ? What is to happen if so many of our merchant ships are sunk that we cannot bring in the food we need to nourish our brave people ? What if the supplies of war materials and war weapons which the United States are seeking to send us in such enormous quantities should in large part be sunk on the way ? What is to happen then ? In February, as you may remember, that bad man in one of his raving outbursts threatened us with a terrifying increase in the numbers and activities of his U-boats and in his air attack—not only on our island but, thanks to his use of French and Norwegian harbours, and thanks to the denial to us of the

Irish bases—upon our shipping far out into the Atlantic. We have taken and are taking all possible measures to meet this deadly attack, and we are now fighting against it with might and main. That is what is called 'the Battle of the Atlantic, which, in order to survive, we have got to win on salt water just as decisively as we had to win the Battle of Britain last August and September in the air.

Wonderful exertions have been made by our Navy and Air Force ; by the hundreds of mine-sweeping vessels which with their marvellous appliances keep our ports clear in spite of all the enemy can do ; by the men who build and repair our immense fleets of merchant ships ; by the men who load and unload them ; and, need I say, by the officers and men of the Merchant

> 'Nothing that is happening now is comparable in gravity with the dangers through which we passed last year. Nothing that can happen in the East is comparable with what is happening in the West.'

Navy who go out in all weathers and in the teeth of all dangers to fight for the life of their native land and for a cause they comprehend and serve. Still, when you think how easy it is to sink ships at sea and how hard it is to build them and protect them, and when you remember that we have never less than 2,000 ships afloat and three or four hundred in the danger zone ; when you think of the great armies we are maintaining and reinforcing in the East, and of the world-wide traffic we have to carry on ; when you remember all this, can you wonder that it is the Battle of the Atlantic which holds the first place in the thoughts of those upon whom rests the responsibility for procuring the victory ?

It was therefore with indescribable relief that I learned of the tremendous decisions lately taken by the President and people of the United States. The American Fleet and flying-boats have been ordered to patrol the wide waters of the Western hemisphere and to warn the peaceful shipping of all nations outside the combat zone, of the presence of lurking U-boats or raiding cruisers belonging to the two aggressor nations. We British will therefore be able to concentrate

our protecting forces far more upon the routes nearer home and to take a far heavier toll of the U-boats there. I have felt for some time that something like this was bound to happen. The President and Congress of the United States, having newly fortified themselves by contact with their electors, have solemnly pledged their aid to Britain in this war because they deem our cause just and because they know their own interests and safety would be endangered if we were destroyed. They are taxing themselves heavily. They have passed great legislations. They have turned a large part of their gigantic industry to making the munitions which we need. They have even given us or lent us valuable weapons of their own. I could not believe that they would allow the high purposes to

which they have set themselves, to be frustrated and the products of their skill and labour sunk to the bottom of the sea. U-boat warfare as conducted by Germany is entirely contrary to international agreements freely subscribed to by Germany only a few years ago. There is no effective blockade but only a merciless murdering and marauding over wide indiscriminate areas utterly beyond the control of the German sea power. When I said ten weeks ago : ' Give us the tools and we will finish the job ', I meant ' give them to us : put them within our reach '—and that is what it now seems the Americans are going to do. And that is why I feel a very strong conviction that though the Battle of the Atlantic will be long and hard and its issue is by no means yet determined, it has entered upon a more grim but at the same time a far more favourable phase. When you come to think of it, the United States are very closely bound up with us now, and have engaged themselves deeply in giving us moral, material, and within the limits I have mentioned, naval support.

It is just worth while therefore taking a look at both sides of the ocean at the forces which are

facing each other in this awful struggle from which there can be no drawing back.

No prudent and far-seeing man can doubt that the eventual and total defeat of Hitler and Mussolini is certain, in view of the respective declared resolves of the British and American democracies. There are less than 70 million malignant Huns—some of whom are curable and others killable—most of whom are already engaged in holding down Austrians, Czechs, Poles, and the many other ancient races they now bully and pillage. The peoples of the British Empire and of the United States number nearly 200 millions in their homelands and in the British Dominions alone. They possess the unchallengeable command of the oceans and will soon obtain decisive superiority in the air. They have more wealth, more technical resources, and they make more steel, than the whole of the rest of the world put together. They are determined that the cause of freedom shall not be trampled down, nor the tide of world progress turned backwards by the criminal Dictators.

While, therefore, we naturally view with sorrow and anxiety much that is happening in Europe and in Africa and may happen in Asia, we must not lose our sense of proportion and thus become discouraged or alarmed. When we face with a steady eye the difficulties which lie before us, we may derive new confidence by remembering those we have already overcome. Nothing that is happening now is comparable in gravity with the dangers through which we passed last year. Nothing that can happen in the East is comparable with what is happening in the West.

'But westward, look, the land is bright !'

Last time I spoke to you I quoted the lines of Longfellow which President Roosevelt had written out for me in his own hand. I have some other lines, which are less well known but which seem apt and appropriate to our fortunes tonight, and I believe they will be so judged wherever the English language is spoken or the flag of freedom flies :—

For while the tired waves, vainly breaking,
Seem here no painful inch to gain,
Far back, through creeks and inlets making,
Comes silent, flooding in, the main.

And not by eastern windows only,
When daylight comes, comes in the light ;
In front the sun climbs slow, how slowly !
But westward, look, the land is bright !

Saucepans
or
steel helmets

EVERYBODY knows that our normal peacetime standards of living must be cut during a war. Everybody knows that ships must carry war needs; that material and labour must all work for the war effort. But does everybody realise that while a shortage of supplies means inconvenience to the buyer, it must mean hardship to the seller?

All honour then to the great mass of traders who accept the new conditions with good grace.

ISSUED BY

THE BOARD OF TRADE

FIRE GUARDS
get ready!
FIREBOMB FRITZ
is coming over

ORDERS TO BURN! Orders to burn us into defeat! What is Britain's answer? It's this — let Firebomb Fritz come. We, the men and women of Britain's Fire Guard, are ready.

We can stand hours of waiting and watching. We can face the dangers. With our pumps and our sandbags, with our ladders and our improvised shields, we've drilled like guardsmen. And now we know our stuff! Firebomb Fritz *can* be beaten — and we're going to do it!

> **FIRE GUARD TIPS. No. 5.** *Water is valuable in a fire-blitz. A piece of flat wood floating in a bucket will stop loss by splashing.*

BRITAIN
SHALL NOT
BURN!

ISSUED BY THE MINISTRY OF HOME SECURITY

READING AIR PHOTOGRAPHS

Listen on Sunday evening at 6.30 when an R.A.F. Officer will use these official un-retouched pictures to illustrate a talk on how the experts are able to interpret R.A.F. photographs of bomb damage in enemy territory

THE GERMAN NAVAL BASE AT KIEL—

Vertical air photographs forming a mosaic of the port, showing damage done prior to recent heavier raids

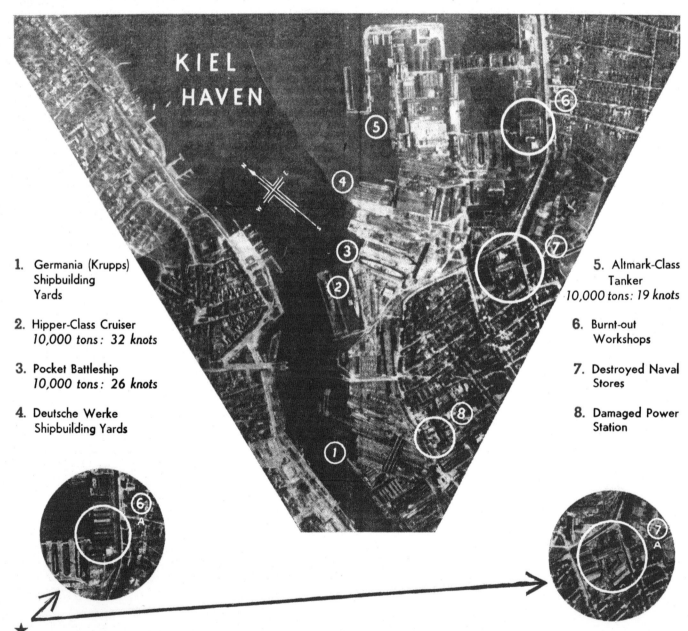

1. Germania (Krupps) Shipbuilding Yards

2. Hipper-Class Cruiser *10,000 tons: 32 knots*

3. Pocket Battleship *10,000 tons: 26 knots*

4. Deutsche Werke Shipbuilding Yards

5. Altmark-Class Tanker *10,000 tons: 19 knots*

6. Burnt-out Workshops

7. Destroyed Naval Stores

8. Damaged Power Station

Insets **6A** and **7A** show the areas marked **6** and **7** before the effect of bomb damage. This small area of Kiel contains some further two hundred examples of damage caused by bombing attacks directed against naval and military objectives in the port

Radio Times, May 2, 1941   Vol. 71   No. 918   Registered at the G.P.O. as a Newspaper

PRICE TWOPENCE

PROGRAMMES FOR May 4 — 10

RADIO TIMES
JOURNAL OF THE BRITISH BROADCASTING CORPORATION
(INCORPORATING WORLD-RADIO)

'The Battle of Britain'

Vapour trails weaving across the sky, the fierce rattle of machine-gun fire—another dog-fight. The story of how the R.A.F. Fighter Command beat the Nazis from the skies of Britain in the great daylight air battles of last autumn is told on Thursday in a dramatic feature written by the author of the Air Ministry best-seller, 'The Battle of Britain'. [Page 20]

ALSO

Samuel Pepys
As 'The Architect of the Navy' (p. 8)

Evelyn Laye
Guest star of 'Monday Night at Eight' (p. 11)

Clifford Evans and Rachel Thomas
In 'Bidden to the Feast', by Jack Jones (p. 11)

Hallé Popular Concerts
Three broadcasts this week (pp. 11, 17, and 23)

'The Island in the Mist'
Favourite Children's Hour serial revived (p. 17)

'Picture-Reporter'
Famous stars in scenes from new films (p. 21)

War Cup Final
Commentary on the second half of the match (p. 24)

Radio Times, June 6, 1941   Vol. 71   No. 923   Registered at the G.P.O. as a Newspaper

PRICE TWOPENCE

PROGRAMMES FOR June 8 — 14

RADIO TIMES
JOURNAL OF THE BRITISH BROADCASTING CORPORATION
(INCORPORATING WORLD-RADIO)

'Ack-Ack, Beer-Beer'
100th BROADCAST

The special show for the men of the Anti-Aircraft batteries and the Balloon Barrage units started on July 1, 1940 and has been broadcast twice a week ever since. A gala programme will celebrate the hundred mark on Thursday this week.

ALSO

PHYLLIS NEILSON-TERRY
In a radio version of 'Trilby' (p. 7 and article p. 3)

MARK HAMBOURG
With Michal Hambourg in 'The BBC Presents—' (p. 8)

JESSIE MATTHEWS
'Monday Night at Eight' (p. 11), 'Old Town Hall' (p.20)

RENEE HOUSTON and DONALD STEWART
'Partnerships' (p. 14), 'Music-Hall' (p. 30)

CHARLES COBORN
This week's 'King-Pin of Comedy' (p. 19)

ERNEST THESIGER
In the radio thriller 'Money with Menaces' (p. 22)

COVERING THE WAR

By 1941, the war was all-encompassing and reflected regularly on *RT's* covers. Among entertainment from performers such as Evelyn Laye and Jessie Matthews, there was the launch of *The Blue Peter* (mentioned below left) — not the later children's TV programme but a radio magazine aimed at the Merchant Navy.

Radio Times, June 27, 1941   Vol. 72   No. 926   Registered at the G.P.O. as a Newspaper

PRICE TWOPENCE

PROGRAMMES FOR June 29 — July 5

RADIO TIMES
JOURNAL OF THE BRITISH BROADCASTING CORPORATION
(INCORPORATING WORLD-RADIO)

'BEYOND VIMY'. The mighty ramparts of the Canadian War Memorial dominate Vimy Ridge where the Canadian Corps made history in 1917. The special Dominion Day programme to be broadcast on Tuesday looks beyond Vimy to the present day which has again brought Canada to fight at the side of the mother country. The story of Canada's 'Torch of Victory' will be another Dominion Day feature.

ALSO THIS WEEK

John Gielgud
In a 'New Arabian Nights' play (p. 7)

'Command Performance'
Record memories of the first Command show (p. 12)

'The Barber of Seville'
Special production of Rossini's opera (p. 19)

'Happy Days'
With Sarah Churchill and Vic Oliver (p. 14)

'The Tradition of Liberty'
Programme for Independence Day (p. 27)

'The Blue Peter'
New Magazine show for the Merchant Navy (p. 28)

'Dick Turpin'
Start of a serial musical melodrama (p. 30)

Radio Times, September 19, 1941   Vol. 72   No. 938   Registered at the G.P.O. as a Newspaper

PRICE TWOPENCE

PROGRAMMES FOR September 21 — 27

RADIO TIMES
JOURNAL OF THE BRITISH BROADCASTING CORPORATION
(INCORPORATING WORLD-RADIO)

'Navy Blue'

Day in, day out, British ships ply the trade routes from the four corners of the globe protected by the guns of the Royal Navy. 'Navy Blue', a new serial starting next Saturday, tells the story of one such ship and her passengers and crew on an adventurous journey across the Atlantic to Great Britain.

★ ★ ★ ALSO ★ ★ ★

'R.U.R.'
Karel Capek's play about the Robots (p. 7)

'Ziegfeld Girl'
Part 1 of the radio version of the film (p. 11)

'White Rajah'
Programme for the centenary of Sarawak (p. 14)

'The Seraglio'
Broadcast of Mozart's opera (p. 19)

Tommy Handley
Starts a new 'ITMA' series (p. 27)

'The Eyes of Britain'
A day with the men of Coastal Command (p. 77)

Saturday 'Music-Hall'
Popular show back to its old place (p. 30)

MURPHY

DOING OUR LEVEL BEST ON TWO FRONTS

We have made up our minds about 1941. The first call on our energies and materials must be for Service requirements. The fact then 'sticks out' that however much we want to, we just shan't be able to produce anything like the number of Murphy Sets that will be needed in the coming months by civilians in their Wardens' Posts, Fire Stations and in their homes. What we can *try* to do is to see that those who have Wireless Sets already are well looked after. A Murphy Set, properly treated, has many years of good life in it. Your Murphy dealer is the man to keep your set going for you and we shall be behind him to see that he can give you the service you need. Your Murphy Set may have to last you a long time. Give it a fair chance by asking your Murphy dealer to *keep* it in good order.

BBC DANCING CLUB

Bandleader and dance expert Victor Silvester launched his *BBC Dancing Club* in July 1941, in an "endeavour to bring the glamour and elegance of good ballroom dancing into your homes". He gave a few minutes of instruction – aided by diagrams of the steps published in *Radio Times* – followed by a concert of music for listeners to dance along to, played by his Ballroom Orchestra. Ballroom dancing, he told *RT*, "helps people take their minds off their troubles and worries, and gives them a chance of stepping forth into a gay, colourful atmosphere. That, as any mind doctor will tell you, is a mental tonic."

The weekly programme ran for two decades on BBC Radio, and expanded into *Television Dancing Club,* which aired on BBC TV from 1948 until 1964.

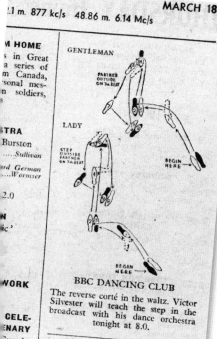

MARCH 18

.1 m. 877 kc/s   48.86 m. 6.14 Mc/s

BBC DANCING CLUB

The reverse corté in the waltz. Victor Silvester will teach the step in the broadcast with his dance orchestra tonight at 8.0.

7.30 SPORTS NEWS FROM CANADA

High lights of the week's Canadian and American sports, prepared for Canadians overseas by the CBC National News Service, and read by

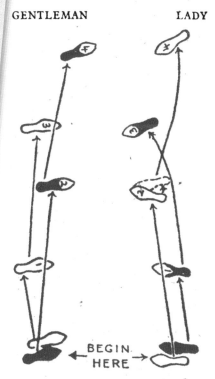

GENTLEMAN   LADY

BEGIN HERE

BBC DANCING CLUB

Here is a diagram of the steps in the open promenade in the tango that Victor Silvester will teach tonight at 8.0.

GENTLEMAN   LADY

BEGIN HERE

BBC DANCING CLUB

In his broadcast tonight at 8.0 Victor Silvester will deal with the zig-zag and backward lock in the quickstep. Here is a diagram of the steps.

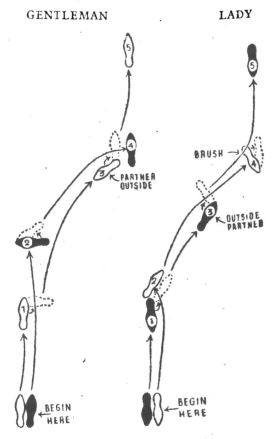

GENTLEMAN   LADY

BRUSH →

PARTNER OUTSIDE

OUTSIDE PARTNER

BEGIN HERE   BEGIN HERE

BBC DANCING CLUB

Here is a diagram of the zig-zag in the Quickstep which Victor Silvester will teach tonight at 8.0.

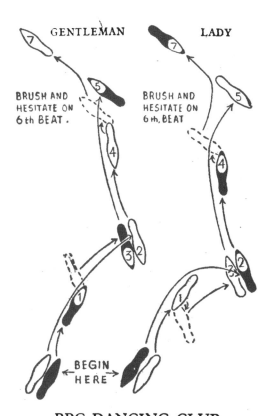

GENTLEMAN   LADY

BRUSH AND HESITATE ON 6th BEAT.   BRUSH AND HESITATE ON 6th BEAT

BEGIN HERE

BBC DANCING CLUB

The hesitation change in the waltz is the step for tonight at 8.0.

Radio Times, December 19, 1941   Vol. 73   No. 951   Registered at the G.P.O. as a Newspaper

PRICE TWOPENCE

PROGRAMMES FOR
Christmas Week

RADIO TIMES
JOURNAL OF THE BRITISH BROADCASTING CORPORATION
(INCORPORATING WORLD-RADIO)

HANDEL'S 'MESSIAH'
Performed by the Hallé Chorus
and Orchestra (Sunday)

GREETINGS TO JOSEPH STALIN
—with a birthday programme of
Russian music (Sunday)

'ANY QUESTIONS?'
Brains Trust in seasonable me
(Sunday and Thursday)

'NO, NO, NANETTE!'
Radio version of the popular
musical comedy (Monday)

'BETHLEHEM'
Rutland Boughton's choral drama
of the Nativity (Monday)

'CHRISTMAS CAVALCADE'
Romantic musical play of
family life (Tuesday)

'MAKE AND MEND'
New magazine programme for the
Navy (Tuesday Forces)

'OLYMPUS TO DINNER'
The Ponsonbys entertain strange
guests (Wednesday)

'UNTO US A CHILD IS BORN'
A Christmas message in words
and music (Wednesday)

THE FIRST CHRISTMAS

*Arise, shine; for thy light is come, and the glory of the Lord is
risen upon thee. For, behold, the darkness shall cover the earth,
and gross darkness the people : but the Lord shall arise upon
thee, and his glory shall be seen upon thee.*

The first of a cycle of plays—'The Man Born to be King'
—will be broadcast on Sunday afternoon. These plays by
Dorothy L. Sayers, introduced in an article on page 5 by
the BBC Director of Religious Broadcasting, represent
probably the first dramatisation of the life of Our Lord
to be broadcast in any country.

'TO ABSENT FRIENDS'
Greetings to the Forces of the
Empire and the Allies (Thursday)

'GOOD WILL AMONG MEN'
Britain and America exchange
Christmas messages (Thursday)

'MOTHER RILEY'
Lucan and McShane invite you to
their Christmas party (Thursday)

CHILDREN CALLING HOME
From Canada, South Africa, and
the U.S.A. (Thursday)

'SNOW WHITE'
Radio version of the Walt Disney
film (Thursday Forces)

'DICK WHITTINGTON'
With Will Fyffe and Harry
Gordon (Thursday Forces)

'PETER PAN'
A Boxing Day broadcast for
young and old (Friday)

'RETURN OF
Ra
fam

'J
Wit
Eva

'THE THIRD CHRISTMAS'

BY LOUIS MACNEICE

NINETEEN-THIRTY-NINE. Nineteen-Forty. Forty-One. This is the third year that Christmas has been dark. In town and country you have to grope for your door. Inside your house it may—or may not—be festive ; outside it remains the same—the same for all, the same as last year—uniformly, ominously dark.

And there were in the same country shepherds abiding in the field, keeping watch over their flock by night . . .

The passages of the Bible describing the first Christmas are still read—aloud or in silence. For the nineteen-hundred-and-forty-first anniversary.

And the glory of the Lord shone round about them.

But that was in Bethlehem and a long time ago.

How do I find my way from here ?

Find your way where to ?

Where do you think ? Home !

Oh, so you've still got one.

Yes I have, but it's not what it was. We've got the glass put back in the windows but there's still a hole in the roof and it looks kind of untidy. Besides, they're all away.

They're all away ? Who are ?

Who do you think ? All my family. Barring my old woman. And *she's* a bit of a trial these days . . . taken to talking in her sleep. Bombing upset her, you know, and losing our Albert in Crete . . . and she says she misses the kiddies—that's our Nellie's children that's gone away to the country . . . it's only nature, I suppose, but she does go on so . . . mumbling and moaning in her sleep. . . .

. . . Now Albert, now Nellie, don't you go making such a noise or Santa Claus won't come down the chimney. Albert, you get back into bed, you'll wake up Jimmy. . . . Jimmy's in Libya. What's the idea sending Jimmy ? He can't even talk yet, he's only a baby. . . .

Oh you do, do you, Nellie ? You want a doll's tea-set ? Well

I don't know, I'm sure. What else do you want, may I ask ? Maybe you think your Dad's a millionaire. . . .

* * * *

Well, that's the way it is ; she talks away in her sleep as if they was still babies. But *they* ain't no babies. Look at Nellie now—let alone Jimmy and Albert. Nellie's sent her kids to the country and works full time in munitions. *She* don't get no time for a spree—not even at Christmas. It's no doll's tea-sets now. Lord, when I think of the old days. . . .

* * * *

Christmas in the old days. A chain of lights through English history. A tradition of bright lights, of roaring fires, and laughter, and songs. It remained for us to encounter Christmas in the blackout.

The bright lights now are shaded but what of the so-called 'Christmas spirit' ? Do those words mean anything, or is that conception as out of date as roasted crabs in the wassail-bowl ? Maybe, you say, it *is* out of date, this Christmas spirit. What about that famous text : 'On earth peace, good will toward men' ? *It's* a bit out of date, surely ?

Do you mean the peace or the good will ? Good will, I think, is the more important, and it's good will that's the essence of Christmas. Those highly coloured cards—though you won't get many this year—showing the child in the manger among those serene beasts —well, often those pictures are a bit sentimental but they do express a necessary human impulse ; the Christian tradition has fostered this impulse but the Dictators would like to crush it—it's the impulse to be generous and gentle towards other living creatures. You notice that Christmas in the modern world has become more and more a festival for the children ? This wasn't its primary purpose but it does serve to remind us that the Christian outlook, unlike the outlook of Nazis and Fascists, does require the grown-up human being to retain the virtues of the child—the child's faith in life and the child's gaiety.

* * * *

Gaiety ? Where do you think you are ? The Middle Ages ? Soon you'll start talking about Yule logs. Look around you, man. That house four doors up made a shot at being gay last year —they had a Christmas tree and all and candles they'd saved from 1938. Nice lot of people they were, too. Well, look at their house

now—you can see the sky through it. 'Hark, the herald angels sing !' Herald angels ! Sirens more likely. . . .

And it came to pass in those days, that there went out a decree from Cæsar Augustus, that all the world should be taxed. . . . And all went to be taxed, every one into his own city.

Government interference with movements of individuals. Registration and classification. . . .

Think of the time we waste filling up forms ! What kind of life is that for a busy woman like me ? And having to queue-up in the food-shops—and nothing so hot when you get it. If it was just for myself I couldn't be bothered, but Bill's coming home for Christmas and so is Nora. Have to do what we can, I suppose. . . . Make them a Christmas pudding with carrots. As for my husband, I must take his mind off those bells.

What bells ? There aren't any bells.

That's just it. He's **a** campanologist.

Eh ?

* * * *

That means he makes a hobby of bells—church bells, you know, preferably old ones—he's learnt up the science of it, knows all the changes you can play on them. He used to be a bell-ringer himself —one time he rang for eight hours on end, came home nearly dead but as proud as Punch. Crazy about church bells like some people are about golf—I suppose people's husbands have to have something like that. Anyway, it's broken his heart. Especially on Christmas Day and New Year's Eve. He keeps reciting bits of poetry about it. . . .

> The time draws near the birth of Christ ;
> The moon is hid ; the night is still ;
> The Christmas bells from hill to hill
> Answer each other in the mist.

Oh no they don't, mate ; least I hope not. We don't want to hear them bells, not while this —— war's on.

Coo, it wouldn't half give me a turn if they did ring. It'd be like seeing a ghost.

Ghost, eh ? Don't you talk to me about ghosts. I saw one myself only yesterday.

You saw a ghost ?

Wasn't in the black-out neither. Broad daylight it was. I'm just walking up High Street and I

happen to look into O'Reilly's window——

Half a mo' ! What did you——?

You know O'Reilly's shop ? Sells sweets and tobacco. Well, I look into the window and what do I see ?—the whole ruddy window plumb full of chocolates and toffees and packets of fifty cigarettes, yes, and crackers, mind you, crackers ! It was the crackers finished me. I go right into the shop, and there's O'Reilly standing behind the counter beaming all over his face. 'What's the game, Mick ? ' I say, ' I know them packets of fags are dummies but where did you get all them sweets ? And where the blazes ', I

say, ' did you get them boxes of crackers ? Or are they dummies too ? ' I say.

'Dummies ? ' says O'Reilly. ' Pull one ! ' and he reaches me a cracker over the counter. It's one of that tough kind that don't give way too easy, and O'Reilly wants to get a better purchase, so he slips his hand almost down to the middle of the cracker instead of just holding the end of it. ' Hey ! ' I say, ' That's not cricket, O'Reilly ', and I grab for the middle, too, and our hands meet. Well ?

* * * *

Well, . . . Well, when I touch his hand it just don't feel like a hand and suddenly I remember . . . . But I look him in the eye and his eyes are still twinkling. ' Merry Christmas, Jack ! ' he says, and the cracker falls away from his hand, and the silver paper, and the jars of sweets vanish, and there's nothing there but the empty shell of the shop that was blown to bits last March and O'Reilly with it. But somehow I feel better.

Why ?

I reckon it was O'Reilly saying ' Merry Christmas ! ' I think them words mean something. Even though he *was* a ghost. . . . Yes, I reckon they mean something.

1942

Radio Times, January 2, 1942 Vol. 74 No. 953 Registered at the G.P.O. as a Newspaper

PRICE TWOPENCE

PROGRAMMES FOR
January 4 — 10

RADIO ✴ TIMES
JOURNAL OF THE BRITISH BROADCASTING CORPORATION
(INCORPORATING WORLD-RADIO)

This Week

Ta-ran-ta-ra!
A radio version of the rollicking Savoy opera *The Pirates of Penzance*, still a favourite after sixty years, will be heard on Sunday, with Derek Oldham as Frederic, Percy Heming as Major-General Stanley, George Baker as the Pirate King, and Robert Easton as the Sergeant of Police.

The 'Bounty'
An authentic account of the mutiny in the *Bounty* is given in the play by Cyril Nash to be broadcast on Sunday.
In 1789, seventeen months after sailing from Portsmouth, William Bligh stood in a small launch and watched his ship in charge of mutineers sail out of sight. With brilliant seamanship he sailed the overloaded launch 3,618 miles to safety.
Of the mutineers, some were found at Tahiti, but of Christian Fletcher, who set out to hide from the world, nothing was heard for eighteen years.

'Man in the Iron Mask'
The identity of the 'man in the iron mask', that lonely figure of the Bastille, will always be a matter for conjecture. In his historical detective story to be broadcast on Monday John Dickson Carr offers a possible solution of the mystery.

More Maugham
Somerset Maugham's stories have proved themselves ideal subjects for radio plays. One that has already been broadcast, 'The Door of Opportunity', will be repeated on Tuesday.
It tells the story of Alban Torel, who had all the attributes for a successful colonial career but one—faced with a crisis, he fell back on the comforting thought that 'courage is the obvious virtue of the stupid'.

Pantomimes
The microphone gives you a front seat at three pantomimes this week—on Monday *The Babes in the Wood* (with Jimmy Nervo and Teddie Knox as particularly bloodthirsty robbers), on Friday *Mother Goose*, and on Saturday *Cinderella*.

Exchange of Views
Religious leaders in Britain and the United States are speaking in a series of talks on Wednesday nights to be broadcast simultaneously in both countries.
In opening the series this week the Archbishop of York speaks on the question of 'What are the underlying spiritual issues of the present crisis and what is the attitude of the Churches to them? An American point of view will be broadcast the following Wednesday.

Marriott and Moffatt
The cheeky fat boy and the cunning old man of so many popular films—Moore Marriott and Graham Moffatt — cause 'A Slight Delay' on Wednesday when they start a radio series. See the article on page 3.

Tudor First Nights'
An unusual series of programmes under this title starts on Wednesday. Listeners will be able to rub shoulders with the crowds at famous first nights in that great period of the English theatre when Shakespeare, Ben Jonson, and Christopher Marlowe were its glittering stars.
The first of these theatrical occasions will be the opening performance of Marlowe's *Tamburlaine*. A commentator in modern style sets the scene, describes the eager pit, the overflowing galleries, the swells with their sixpenny stools on the stage, and takes his microphone eavesdropping among the audience.

AMERICA AND THE SEA
Another American ship slides into the water to help the Allied cause. 'America Turns Again to the Sea', to be broadcast on Thursday, tells the story of the American Merchant Marine set against a background of the clamour of her shipyards of today, which all around her long coastline are singing so furious a song.

Convoy
Two programmes this week bring listeners thrilling and authentic pictures of the work of the Navy in protecting Britain's convoys.
On Wednesday (Forces) the guns will be heard in action against enemy aircraft when Bob Dougall's recorded commentary made on board a destroyer on escort duty with an East Coast convoy is broadcast.
On Friday '30 Degrees West', by George Blake, written with the co-operation of the Admiralty, presents a dramatic account of convoy work in the Atlantic.

Unusual Plays
Two plays by Norman Edwards to be broadcast on Saturday have strange stories to tell. *The Dancers*, adapted from a story by Eric Linklater, tells of the fate of a picnic party. *The Dappled Farm* reveals the remarkable reason for the breaking off of an engagement.

Handley Panto
Tommy Handley and some of the ITMA gang, aided and abetted by Vera Lennox and Charles Penrose, are giving a special pocket pantomime for the children on Saturday afternoon.

MASTERS OF THE SEAS

ABOVE in January 1942, *Radio Times* reported, "Another American ship slides into the water to help the Allied cause."

MAIN PICTURE in September, the BBC Home Service aired *Launching a Walrus*, billed as "an outside broadcast from a naval station somewhere in Britain."

LAUNCHING A 'WALRU
microphone takes you to a Na
are catapulted

...rom the deck of **H.M.S.** *Warspite.* The
Station today at 1.15 to hear how aircraft
ships of the Royal Navy.

VIC OLIVER MAROONED

Tonight at 8.0 in the first of a new series, 'Desert Island Discs', he will tell you about the eight records he would choose to keep himself entertained if he were condemned to spend the rest of his life on a desert island.

8.0 'DESERT ISLAND DISCS'

1—Vic Oliver discusses with Roy Plomley the eight records he would choose if he were condemned to spend the rest of his life on a desert island with a gramophone for his entertainment

The old question as to which few books you would select for company on a desert island has been thoroughly thrashed out. Now—given those necessities of an unbreakable gramophone and an endless supply of needles—the problem of musical diversion is to be discussed. Certainly the problem is not an easy one, and only the very greatest music of its type can stand the test of time and repetition.

In the weeks ahead numbers of famous folk will play you their idea of what records will stand these tests. James Agate, dramatic critic, comes next week, to be followed the week after by one who should speak with authority on desert islands—Commander A. B. Campbell.

DESERT ISLAND DISCS

A radio classic was born on Thursday 29 January 1942, when the very first edition of *Desert Island Discs* was transmitted on the BBC's For the Forces network. The castaway was Vic Oliver, an actor, comedian and the star of BBC radio's *Hi, Gang!* Roy Plomley, the deviser and host of *Desert Island Discs*, would remain in charge until his death 43 years later in 1985. His show is still running in the 21st century...

OPPOSITE PAGE a forgotten favourite of the 1940s was *In Britain Now*, a Home Service magazine show with "its finger on the endless pulse of life".

IN BRITAIN NOW

Geoffrey Grigson writes about an old favourite that for the weeks ahead takes the place of 'The World Goes By'

MOLE-CATCHING in the Midlands; a handcuff-maker from Birmingham; pit-ponies from Wales; a village in the Highlands; a riveter from Clydeside—do you remember 'In Britain Now'? This weekly talks magazine is now back in the programmes. It is broadcast from 6.45 to 7.15 every Wednesday evening in the Home Service, and it began on March 4.

Thirty minutes. For you, thirty comfortable minutes in front of

FRANK GILLARD, war correspondent, compères the show

the fire, as your wireless takes you from Cornish valleys to Scottish mountains. For us who produce the magazine, thirty rather anxious minutes. Some half-dozen men and women will be waiting in studios all over the country, with an eye on the clock and the red light which warns them of their turn. In another studio at a BBC headquarters sits Frank Gillard, waiting to introduce to you, one by one, these invisible talkers hundreds of miles away. And engineers will also be standing by, to hook up from one studio to the next. There are 1,800 seconds in that thirty minutes, and each of them matters.

Every week 'In Britain Now' is the climax of several weeks. Weeks of travelling, planning, interviewing, telephoning. Weeks of fitting together a jig-saw made of hundreds of small awkward bits. Speakers cannot be found by sitting in an office. Factories must be visited. Workshops, canteens, rivers, islands. One day the Talks Assistant may be trudging over the

farm in gum-boots in search of a farmer, another day putting on dungarees to protect himself from the drip of a Cornish tin-mine. One day he breathes sea air, another Black Country smoke.

All the while his quarry is the man or woman with a good story to tell, and a good clear local voice to tell it with. For 'In Britain Now' is two things at once. It is national and local. In war the local side of national life gets a bit squashed out. Newspapers have not so much room for local news. Broadcasting cannot reflect local life in the old ample way. But neither war nor Whitehall can turn a Yorkshireman into a Welshman or vice-versa. And that's where 'In Britain Now' comes in. It gives local life, war effort, morale a chance to speak nationally.

'In Britain Now' will tell Britain something of what's on, north, south, east, and west. Not only the war things that are on, although naturally a lot about them for the war colours everything today. But a laugh, a bit of fun, a bit of escape, are not merely permissible in wartime—they are necessary.

Work and Play

Moscow kept its theatres going when the Nazis could see the Kremlin through their field-glasses. Very well. 'In Britain Now' will relax. Talkers will sometimes tell you about their play, their hobbies, and so on, as well as about their jobs and their war-service. Sometimes they will tell you about a local custom still kept up, or recall a local man still remembered, who did great things in the past. Sometimes the recording car will go out where things are done and bring a factory or a quarry or a school or a camp into the bill. Sometimes you may get a description of some town or village or building, or some place famous for its scenery or associations. Maybe a talker may come from a research station which keeps an eye on farming or wartime food, and maybe a refugee from another country may talk of his impressions of this Britain now. No two human beings are alike. That's the point. A Prime Minister may knit for a hobby or fell trees, or the sub-editor of railway time-tables keep living sea-anemones in his flat.

The well cannot go dry—that's the fun of 'In Britain Now'. It will have its finger on the endless variation of life.

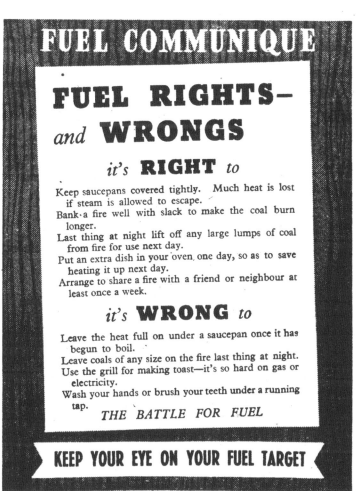

THE CITY OF WASHINGTON

'THE YOUNG MR. PITT'

A radio version of the Twentieth-Century Fox film will be broadcast on Sunday, with Robert Donat (above) and Robert Morley as Charles James Fox, playing their original film parts

ROLL OF HONOUR

In July 1942, *RT* depicted outstanding workers on the War Front featured in *Award for Industry* on For the Forces. In August, on the Home Service, Robert Donat starred in a radio version of his hit film *The Young Mr Pitt*.

PRODUCTION FRONT

ROLL OF HONOUR

The weekly 'Award for Industry' broadcast on Sundays brings to the microphone men and women chosen to represent the magnificent effort of the workers on Britain's 'production front'. Here are those who were introduced to listeners in the first six of these broadcasts.

MRS. ALICE WATTS, *assistant forewoman in a shell-filling factory in the North West of England. She has six daughters, two working in the same factory as herself.* (Broadcast on June 14)

MRS. CLARA HALL *was formerly a tailoress. She has risen from the lowest-grade worker in a Yorkshire Royal Ordnance Factory to become shop supervisor. She is the mother of three children.* (Broadcast on July 5)

FRED SHEPLEY, *skilled engineer and foreman of the tool room in a Royal Ordnance Factory in the Midlands. He was a mechanic in the Royal Flying Corps during the last war and has done over six hundred hours' flying, testing engines.* (Broadcast on June 21)

RICHARD HARRIS *comes from a farming family but has worked in the aircraft industry for ten years. In his spare time he is an Air Training Corps instructor.* (Broadcast on June 28)

MRS. EDITH FOSTER, *who was chosen to take part in the first of these programmes on May 31, is a 'leading hand' in an ordnance factory. She has a baby girl.*

MRS. ROSE JACKMAN *bends pipes for Spitfires. She has been in the same factory for six years.* (Broadcast on June 7)

MEETING 'UNCLE SAM AT WAR'

Alistair Cooke has cabled us this prefatory note to his new series starting on Sunday evening

THE series of six feature programmes that begins on Sunday is an attempt to tell you in dramatic form what war has done to ordinary people in some of the different regions of the United States.

This series was conceived a year ago and commissioned by the BBC before Pearl Harbour, but it is a happy coincidence that it should be in production just when Norman Corwin is dramatising for Americans a similar tribute to the people of Great Britain. After December 7 we drastically revised the scope of the series and themes to be dramatised.

I drove out of New York City on a crisp cold day at the end of February. I had along with me Theodore Lawrence, a fine recording engineer, and my intention was to record people everywhere and let them speak in their own accents with their own language, then return to New York with this material and edit it. My point was mainly to avoid a besetting sin of radio everywhere—namely, the assumption that professional actors who live and have their interests in a metropolis can at the drop of a director's wrist easily enact any type of national character. I have always noticed how alternately amused and disgusted is a Texan or a southerner, or a Chicago broker, when he comes to New York and sees himself grotesquely misrepresented.

However, this noble impulse to substitute a slice of truth for the *ersatz* characters that actors create soon had a rough encounter with facts of life. I got my Floridans and Kentuckians and Texans, but we had to record them in strange places. Their accents were very hard indeed for English ears to follow, and the moment the microphone appeared it was like a dagger at their throats. Before long we revised all our plans. It was evident we would have to sacrifice that well-cooked slice of truth in the cause of finding some sort of reasonable legitimate food you would be able to digest. So from Texas on I went alone, and the rest of the time it was using the eyes, the legs, the ears and a small library of notebooks. These were all—I'm happy to say—brought back safely to New York City after a journey that took me wriggling round four corners of the United States.

The only other purpose that needs mentioning here is a determination not to feed you with a lot of inspirational hokum. Americans are good at dramatising their work and play, even when that work and play is a waste of time. Better than any other race on earth the British can accept painful and humdrum truth without a chorus of rah, rah, rahs. So I have tried to avoid faking anybody's motives or falsely representing every living American as puffing and panting for love of Britain, Russia, and China. Charles Schenck, who directed all six of these scripts, has borne nobly with me in this ambition, and we have tried to make actors stop sounding like actors and sound like people. We hope they will sound so to you, and that some of them will be people you will like to know.

ALISTAIR COOKE

Broadcasting legend Alistair Cooke had been reporting on America for the BBC since 1935. After a pilot show in June 1942, his programme *Uncle Sam at War* aired fortnightly from 30 August. His series *Letter from America* would run until his death in 2004.

Planning Your Listening—Nazi Version

A BOOK published in Berlin called *Der Rundfunk als Führungsmittel* or The Wireless as a Means of Dictatorship), written by a good partymember by the name of Eckert, presents a complete exposition of the function of broadcasting as conceived by the Nazi state.

One passage should interest particularly all those whose wise regular habit it is to use the RADIO TIMES as it is meant to be used: Eckert deplores any publication of radio programmes in advance, because 'they may enable the listener to choose only those items which particularly interest him. . . . Nothing is so barbarous as the liberalistic way of picking out such broadcasts as happen to appeal to the mood of the moment.'

So now you know, all you millions of British listeners who plan your listening in advance : you are being barbarous and liberalistic. Just another manifestation, this, of the Nazi principle of simple inversion by which black becomes white and white black, to serve the corrupt ends of party dictatorship.

Before the advent of the Nazis to power the German Government of the day published a statement of their aims in regard to broadcasting. 'The German wireless', they announced, ' is the servant of the German people. It serves no political party. All political matters must be objectively treated.'

Goebbels soon changed all that. He recognised the enormous potential power of the broadcast word. Other countries, other broadcasting organisations, including the BBC, have set themselves deliberately to harness that power, taking steps to counteract the danger of letting loose a new kind of demagogue, the radio demagogue. It was always foreseen that, given the chance, a man might sway the destiny of the world for good or evil simply because he is a good broadcaster, not because what he says is right. Men like Father Coughlin in America have tasted something of this power (it would be tactless, perhaps, to try to find examples nearer home). But the point is that no one in America is obliged to listen to Father Coughlin. Listeners can pick and choose. They can hear equally powerful speakers presenting views directly opposite to those of Father Coughlin.

Goebbels allows you no choice—not even, in theory, the right to switch off. It is not enough, says Eckert, to prevent the German public from listening to foreign transmissions ; they must listen to the German wireless with appropriate emotions. Communal listening is therefore to be encouraged at the expense of private listening. Broadcasts designed to appeal to the individual listener are not sufficiently totalitarian. What is wanted is the mass response to a mass appeal.

Communal listening is particularly important for the Hitler Youth, because it forces the individual to subordinate his will to that of the community. He cannot simply go out of the room or turn the wireless off and on when he wants, but has to listen to the broadcast with the others. *We thus teach the growing children to use the wireless correctly.*

Thus in broadcasting as in all else the ideal of the Nazi is pitched lower, infinitely lower, than that of any other community. Exploitation is substituted for enlightenment. Instead of probing for truth, they rejoice in hammering home a lie.

Among the many greater things the world of free men is fighting for we must not forget to include the right to choose our radio programmes in advance.

GORDON STOWELL

> **'Among the many greater things the world of free men is fighting for, we must not forget to include the right to choose our programmes in advance'**

The BBC Microphone

THIS microphone with the BBC label figures prominently nowadays in most photographs of British broadcasters in action. The device was introduced only a year or so ago when such photographs, or reproductions of them, began to be sent abroad in considerable quantities.

Its introduction represented the expression of a legitimate pride; for the BBC microphone had already begun to command not only the attention but the respect of the world. Those three letters 'B B C' have now come to be recognised in every part of the world as a symbol and a synonym for truth as surely as the swastika has come to be recognised as the symbol of all that is crooked and cruel.

As Mr. Robert Foot, Joint Director-General of the BBC, said in opening the 'BBC at War' Exhibition at Glasgow earlier this month:

Britain's radio voice has always set the seal of truth. Its news bulletins, read in 22 European languages and 46 altogether in the world service, proceed, all of them, from the same foundation—the foundation of truth. There may be 46 languages, but there is only one BBC; and its news bulletins are heard throughout the whole world, and wherever they are heard they are trusted.

Here is an achievement of which all British people may be justly proud. For remember, it was not a foregone conclusion in September 1939. There was no guarantee that the world at large would regard the words of the BBC in any different light from the words of the Nazis. The microphone was an untried weapon of war and there were many ways in which it could have been used or abused. But the BBC was resolved upon the decision that, come what might, its own microphone would be preserved as a vehicle for telling the whole world, allied, neutral, and enemy, nothing but the truth.

Magna est veritas et prevalebit. There is a wisdom in the old tag that has stood the test of centuries. It has nothing in common with the cynical maxim of *Mein Kampf* to the effect that people will believe any lie if only it is made big enough and repeated often enough, a maxim that failed to foresee in the microphone the most sensitive and dispassionate detector of a lie ever known.

That the truth will always prevail is due to this peculiar quality in the microphone and to the inherent power of truth itself. Yet to the BBC must go the credit of ensuring that the truth is now being spread far and wide for all who have ears and the will to hear, not least in those countries ruled or occupied by an enemy so afraid of the truth that those who listen to it must do so in peril of their very lives—yet still do so.

* * * * *

Look for the sign of the BBC microphone each week on this page of the RADIO TIMES. Beneath it you will always find some brief but illuminating sidelight on the vast and varied work of the BBC as it sets itself to its privileged task of serving the people of this country and, indeed, of the world.

> **The BBC was resolved upon the decision that, come what might, its own microphone would be preserved as a vehicle for telling the whole world, allied, neutral, and enemy, nothing but the truth**

'The News will include—'

Frank Gillard, a BBC News Observer, describes his work of collecting and recording news talks and stories

COLLECTING the raw material of a news story is a fascinating game; you never know quite where the trail will lead you. In the last few months I have soared through the air in gliders, walked on the sea bed in a diving suit, and been down clay pits and tin mines. I have visited farms and factories, workshops and dockyards, parade grounds and operations rooms, barges and battleships, and I have talked to every sort of person.

But getting the story is one thing and telling it is quite another, and here a radio reporter comes up against his biggest problem and his greatest opportunity. How are you going to present the story to your listeners? It may be that the best way is a straightforward account of what you have seen and heard, much like a newspaper story. But there is a difference. You are one up on the newspaper man, because as you tell your story over the microphone you give it life with the inflexions of your voice, and you can be more personal when you are talking direct to the audience. On the other hand, you cannot be sure that your voice pleases everybody. Your voice may be a disadvantage, or you may speak the sentences badly. Hence you have to take as much trouble as any skilled craftsman; as you write your account you try it over to make sure of telling the story in such a way that the listener may really listen.

The Mobile Unit

The aim always is to make a story as nearly as possible a first-hand experience for the listener; thus, you are always looking out for better ways of using sound in telling it—and not only the sound of your voice. This is where the mobile recording unit comes in. The folk who make news are often too busy to travel to a studio, so the news observer takes his microphone to them. The recording apparatus fits into half of the back seat of an ordinary car. The luggage boot of the same car carries microphones and hundreds of feet of cable. In this way you can often go out and collect your story in the voice of the man or woman most concerned in it.

It is not always easy. A remarkably high proportion of British heroes are inarticulate, and even the chap who is garrulous enough over a cup of tea or a pint of beer may become tongue-tied when he faces a microphone. The BBC reporter has to talk to his man first, to find out what his story really is. At the same time he is sizing up his voice and style as a broadcaster. If the signs are favourable, the reporter invites his victim to make a recording, helps him to draft what he wants to say, gives him a few simple tips in microphone technique, takes him perhaps through a few trial runs, and then finally passes a cue to the engineer in the car to drop the cutting needle on to the blank disc. The first attempt may be a failure, and a second or third recording may be necessary; but in the end, with patience and persistence all round,

BBC VALUES

An October *RT* showed how the BBC was becoming a beacon of truth around the world. In July, Frank Gillard explained the work of a BBC news reporter.

ON THE JOB

The work of a News Observer takes him to many strange places, as when Frank Gillard visited a Royal Engineers Diving Unit attached to a Port Construction Company. Here he is seen with portable typewriter on his knee, typing the Commanding Officer's script. The C.O. then recorded his descriptive comment. Later Gillard made a descent in a diving-suit and recorded what he saw by means of a microphone in his diver's helmet.

and often some perspiration as well, the job is done.

Sometimes a radio reporter is sent to cover a more complicated event, where he can really let himself go in his use of the recording car. Suppose he is to give listeners an account of night operations at an R.A.F. station. He and his technical colleagues will take the car along to the aerodrome and record whatever useful material may be available—the pilots being briefed, the engines warming up, the machines taking off, perhaps some of the messages coming back on the R-T, pilots reporting on their return, and so on.

Illustrations in Sound

Back in the studio the next morning, he plays these discs over, makes himself familiar with them, and chooses the important parts. Then he records his own account of the night's events, 'dubbing' in flashes of the actuality from these discs as he goes along. In this way he builds up a story which has illustrations—in sound; and the illustrations should come exactly where the listener can get most value from them. The reporter must not be too excited by his illustrations, of course. 'Noises off' may be a great nuisance to the listener if he is not quite sure what they are.

The Home Service bulletins alone are carrying up to eighty or ninety news talks each month. In addition, the BBC's observers are supplying quantities of material every day to the Empire and other overseas bulletins, which go out from London to all parts of the world. In a war such as this, words are weapons; every good reporter believes that honest and straightforward reporting can play a useful part in fighting for victory.

DO YOU REMEMBER THESE COVERS?

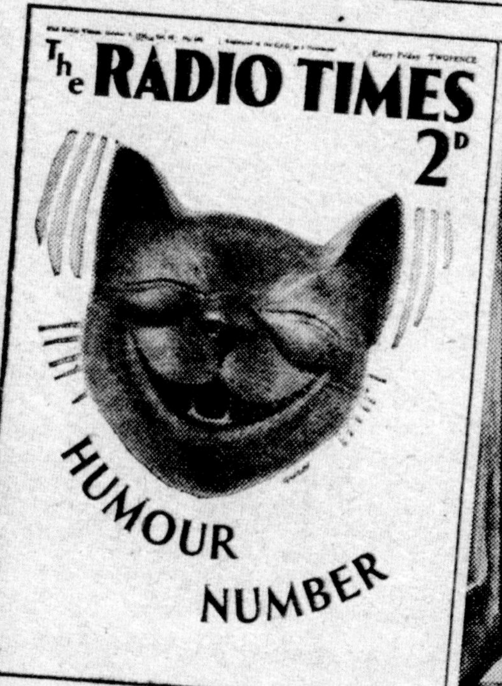

EY REPRESENT some of the milestones in our thousand-number journey. You see the covers of No. 1, the first
ver of all; No. 181, the first of many 'special' numbers, celebrating the Beethoven Centenary in 1927; No. 450, marking
BBC's move to Broadcasting House; No. 680, with Gilroy's memorable cat, which set the whole country laughing in
36; No. 710, the Coronation Number, designed by C. R. W. Nevinson — well over three million copies were sold; and
No. 831A, an historic extra issue that was rushed to press in one day on the eve of Britain's declaration of war.

1,000 ISSUES

With the magazine dated 29 November–5 December 1942, *Radio Times* clocked up its 1,000th issue and marked the occasion with a reminder of some landmark covers.

RADIO ✴ TIMES
JOURNAL OF THE BRITISH BROADCASTING CORPORATION
The war years 1943

1943

BIG W

PASS THE AMMUNITION!

A programme this evening at 7.15 describes the journeys necessary to produce and supply a six-pounder shell

HEELS . . .

PANTO SEASON

New Year 1943 found *Radio Times* in relatively cheery mood, promoting *Aladdin* at the Sheffield Lyceum and *Mother Goose* at the London Coliseum.

his Spitfire . . .

He had dreamed of it—
thought of it—
read of it—
neglected his lessons
for it—
Watched it through the
classroom window.
and now
He'd got it . . .
His own Spitfire!
He had worked hard—
even studied . . .
listened with his eyes
popping, asked
questions, travelled to
Canada—to America
and back home just

HOW THE BBC CALLS ALL NATIONS

'HERE IS THE NEWS'

'Hier, Radio Belgie'

'A estação da BBC. Vai trasmitir o seo 3 boletim'

'Englannin yleisradio Lontoo. Suomenkielinen lähetys alkaa'

'Şimdi Havadis bültenimizi okuyorum'   'Hier volg die Nuus in Afrikaans'

'Aici este postul de Radio Londra. Buna dimineața! Veți auzi acum primul buletin de știri în limba română'

'Ici Radio Belgique'

'Estación de la BBC. Vamos a radiar nuestro boletin de noticias en castellaño'

'Ici Londres.   'Po apım buletinin e   'Parla Londra:
Voici notre bulletin   lajmeve   Prima trasmissione serale
d'informations'   ne giuhén Shqipe'   in lingua italiana'

'Se nxandru issa, it-Tahdida ta Ahbarijiet bil-Malti'   'He aquí las noticias'

'Vola Londýn . . . Vyslechnéte   'De hører BBC's
dneśni zpravy'   aftenudsendelse paa dansk'

'God Morgen. Dette er London med morgennyheiene'

'Dobar den dragi slušateli'   'Aqui estão as noticias'

'Radio London : dajemo prenos porocil
ki ga oddajamo vsaki dan v slovenścini'

'Hier ist England. Hier ist England. Hier ist England'
'Hireket mondunk'

'Dziendobry Państwu.
. . . Brytyjskiego w języku Polskim'

The BBC in Europe

THE MAP reproduced below, which shows at a glance the extent to which the BBC's regular transmissions are heard in the countries of Europe, is part of a special wall-map prepared for the BBC at the request of the Army Bureau of Current Affairs.

The key to the letters is as follows : A—ICELAND, ¼ hr. weekly in Icelandic ; B—NORWAY, 1 hr. 35 mins. daily in Norwegian ; C—SWEDEN, 45 mins. daily in Swedish ; D—FINLAND, 1 hr. daily in Finnish ; E—DENMARK, 1 hr. daily in Danish ; F—HOLLAND, 2 hrs. 15 mins. daily in Dutch ; G—GERMANY, 4 hrs. 10 mins. daily in German, ½ hr. daily special news in Morse ; H—POLAND, 2 hrs. 10 mins. daily in Polish ; I—BELGIUM, 1 hr. 15 mins. daily in French and Flemish ; J—FRANCE, 5 hrs. daily in French, ½ hr. daily special news in Morse ; K—SWITZERLAND receives French, Italian and German Services from BBC daily ; L—AUSTRIA, 1 hr. daily in German ; M—CZECHO-SLOVAKIA, 1 hr. 35 mins. daily in Czech and Slovak ; N—HUNGARY, 1 hr. 15 mins. daily in Hungarian ; O—RUMANIA, 1 hr. 20 mins. daily in Rumanian ; P—SPAIN, 1 hr. 15 mins. daily in Spanish, PORTUGAL, 1 hr. daily in Portuguese ; Q—CORSICA and SARDINIA receive BBC French and Italian ; Services daily ; R—ITALY, 4 hrs. 15 mins. daily in Italian ; S—YUGO-SLAVIA, 1 hr. 35 mins. daily in Serbo-Croat, ½ hr. daily in Slovene ; T—BULGARIA, 45 mins. daily in Bulgarian ; U—ALBANIA, 25 mins. daily in Albanian ; V—GREECE, 1 hr. 45 mins. daily in Greek ; W—TURKEY, 1 hr. daily in Turkish ; X—CYPRUS, ½ hr. weekly special service in Greek ; Y—MALTA, ½ hr. weekly special service in Maltese.

In all these countries the BBC Home Service and/or short-wave Empire Services in English are also received.

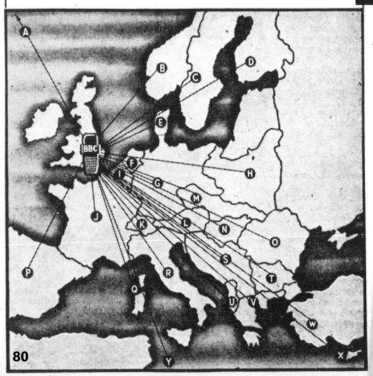

The Royal Message to the BBC

BUCKINGHAM PALACE

I send my hearty congratulations to the British Broadcasting Corporation on the twenty-first anniversary of its foundation.

In peace and war alike, it has proved itself a great national institution, rendering high service to the State and to millions of listeners all over the world.

I wish the Corporation all success in the future, when broadcasting will play a part of ever-increasing importance in the lives of all of us.

George R.I.

14th November 1943.

eric fraser

WAR AND PEACE

On 17 January 1943, the BBC began its first ever full-cast dramatisation of Tolstoy's classic novel. Serialised in eight parts for the Home Service, it starred Celia Johnson as Natasha Rostov and Leslie Banks as Pierre Bezukhov. Eric Fraser provided illustrations for *Radio Times*.

'WAR AND PEACE'

of
'ar
ice
—
ar-
ss
of a
ng

ar ',
nse
ks,
en's

s of
ida-
by
xist-
ned
sent
the
me ;
rris,
ent,
say

Radio Times, February 26, 1943 Vol. 78 No. 1013 Registered at the G.P.O. as a Newspaper

PRICE TWOPENCE

RADIO ✹ TIMES
JOURNAL OF THE BRITISH BROADCASTING CORPORATION
(INCORPORATING WORLD-RADIO)

Special Programmes

This week will be broadcast a sequence of over fifty programmes designed to present a composite picture of the British Army, and of its development from the sombre days of the campaign which ended at Dunkirk to the present day which finds it a tremendous fighting machine armed and poised for the grim tasks ahead.

Echo of Agincourt

Several of Sunday's programmes will prelude the official sequence ; in the afternoon will be broadcast scenes from Shakespeare's *King Henry the Fifth*, with Esmond Knight in the part of the warrior-king. In 1415 the men wore armour, and in 1943 the armour is borne by the vehicles, but the same spirit informs the steel.

Official Opening

On Sunday night, after the nine o'clock news, Sir James Grigg, Secretary of State for War, will come to the microphone to introduce the sequence. After his talk listeners will hear recorded messages from the following commanders : General Sir Bernard Paget (Home Forces), General Sir George Giffard (West Africa), Lt.-General Sir William Platt (East Africa), Field Marshal Sir Archibald Wavell (India), General Sir Henry Maitland Wilson (Middle East), General the Hon. Sir Harold Alexander (North Africa), Lt.-General Kenneth Anderson (1st Army), Field Marshal the Viscount Gort (Malta), Lt.-General Mason Macfarlane (Gibraltar), and General Sir Alan Brooke (Chief of the Imperial General Staff).

The Building of an Army

Under this title the main series of three programmes—to be heard on Monday, Wednesday, and Friday nights respectively—will present a documented account of the crescendo of events from Munich to Dunkirk, from Dunkirk to Dieppe, and up to and including the Battle of Egypt. The first and second of these programmes were written by Major Eric Linklater and Stephen Potter; the third is by Denis Johnston, lately BBC war correspondent in Egypt.

'On the Job'

Another series, this time of four programmes allotted between Monday, Thursday, Friday, and Saturday, will show units engaged in different sides of army work—one at gun drill in a coastal battery, another carrying out a night exercise at a battle school, a third training as airborne troops, and—as the final programme of the whole week's sequence—a fourth unit relieving its sentries at a London barracks before the sounding of the Last Post.

The Scottish Pipes

On Monday evening a programme called 'Pipes of the Misty Moorland' will recall in the form of dramatised episodes some of the many historical occasions when the sound of the pipes has inspired or accompanied Scottish gallantry in battle.

With the Home Guard

On Tuesday evening men of the Tynemouth Battalion of the Northumberland Home Guard will tell their own story of its formation, training, and duties, typifying the spirit of Britain's 'spare-time army'.

'Song of the Regiment'

Also on Tuesday evening this programme will bring to listeners legends and songs of the Regimental Marches of the British Army. The singers will be Elsie French, Jan van der Gucht, and John Mott.

Changing Guard

Wednesday morning's dismounting and mounting of King's Guard will be broadcast with commentaries.

Following Up

'The Young Idea', a glimpse of the Army Cadet Corps at work, will be presented on Wednesday afternoon.

'Strange but True'

Odd facts about the present-day Army, and strange episodes in the lives of soldiers, will be presented in this programme on Wednesday evening.

'Radio Reconnaissance'

The programme under this heading on Wednesday night will be 'The Army as a Team' and will describe the way in which all arms are used in a battalion.

through the Week

Battlefronts

On Thursday evening a programme by the 'Marching On' team will take listeners in imagination to all the fronts where British soldiers are now to be found.

Settling In

On Saturday evening a programme called 'What! No Morning Tea?' will describe the recruit's first six weeks in the Army.

March Past

The principal programme on Saturday evening will be 'The British Army Marches Past', a panorama of marching feet and gunfire and moving armour, of bugle-calls and music, regimental names and battle-honours.

Bands in the Week

The Army bands to be heard will be the Royal Artillery (Woolwich) Band, the R.A.S.C. Band and Dance Band, the Welsh Guards Band, the Coldstream Guards Band, the Scots Guards Band, the Pipes and Drums of the Army School of Piping, the Blue Rockets Dance Orchestra (R.A.O.C.), the Band of the Bedfordshire and Hertfordshire Regiment, the Electronomes Dance Band, the Royal Artillery Theatre Orchestra, the R.A.M.C. Dance Band, the Band and Dance Band of the Manchester Regiment, the Band of the Loyal Regiment, and the Dance Orchestra of the King's Royal Rifle Corps.

Other Programmes

Sunday morning, an Army Service ; Sunday afternoon, an orchestral concert for members of H.M. Forces ; Sunday evening, 'The Army Sings' (hymn-singing at Cardiff); Monday Night, St. David's Day Concert ; Tuesday afternoon, John Hilton talking ; Tuesday evening, the Brains Trust; Wednesday evening, 'Stand Easy!', a high-speed Variety show by the Troops for the Troops ; Thursday night, War Commentary by Major Lewis Hastings ; Friday evening 'Music

THE MEANING OF ARMY WEEK

Cecil McGivern, producer in charge of the Army Week broadcasts, describes the scope and purpose of this unexampled sequence of programmes devoted to one magnificent theme

'One man—the ordinary British Tommy'

IN the autumn and winter of 1939 the waters of the English Channel whitened round the bows of troop-ships carrying another army away from England. That army sang as all British armies have sung, words relevant to war—'*Roll out the barrel . . . .*'. That army was followed by the pride and tears of a Britain who for years had been conditioned to pacifism—a Britain who for years had made it clear that she had little money to spare for arms and ammunition, a Britain who had not seen the inevitable result of a Germany striving with vast energy to build an unbeatable army.

Yet that British Expeditionary Force was no 'token' army, but a powerful force, trained and equipped as well as we then knew how. But we did not know enough. And when the soldiers of Holland and Belgium and France could fight no more, the B.E.F. had to be brought back across a Channel mercifully calm under the small craft which covered its surface. The Army's equipment was now simply jettisoned impedimenta.

Britain Alone

Then Britain, alone, faced a triumphant Germany and a boastful Italy. And an officer in charge of a unit on the coast of Britain smiled as he read in his orders: 'In the event of no weapons being available for them, officers will cut for themselves stout sticks'.

Then it began—the organising, the recruiting, the training, the equipping. While Dunkirk followed Norway, and Greece followed Dunkirk, and Singapore followed Greece, the new British Army was built. In three years, fighting out of its weight, it grew into a modern aggressive force, matching the armoured divisions, the airborne divisions, the craftsmen infantry of the enemy—matching and finally outmatching them. A new British Army emerged, able to crack wide open the hand-picked Afrika Corps and beat it back over 1,500 miles of desert. That Army—an Army of men who in 1938 had thought of war only to hate it—is now an Army of first-line

soldiers in a war that has given every soldier a complicated and technical job. It looks confidently and eagerly forward to the struggle which will lead to final victory.

That is the thing few other nations could have done, and none could have done it better and more quickly.

Building Up the Week

And that is the story which the BBC sets out to tell in Army Week. At the time of writing, more than fifty programmes have been planned to pay tribute to the British Army; this tribute is probably the biggest project the BBC has undertaken.

The attention of listeners is respectfully drawn to the word 'planned'. This is not simply a collection of programmes put together in one week to give that week an Army flavour. The Planning Department of the BBC, with the full co-operation of the War Office, has seen to it that these programmes have a shape and a design.

The main thread of the story of the British Army and the backbone to the week's programmes are the three broadcasts on Monday, Wednesday, and Friday nights called 'The Building of an Army'. In the first two of these Eric Linklater and Stephen Potter tell the story of the making of an Army from Munich to Dunkirk, and from Dunkirk to Dieppe, the combined operations raid which was—though none of us realised it—the full-scale dress

rehearsal for North Africa. The third of these programmes tells the story of the great victory in Egypt in a dramatisation written by Denis Johnston, just returned from there.

Around these three are built the numerous other programmes—each carefully selected for some good reason. The 'live' broadcasts arranged by the Outside Broadcasting Department take us to the 'Army on the Job'. The Variety programmes are not just entertainment with an Army flavour. In one the Army entertains itself and us—and it can do so because in the long months of training and waiting the Army had to entertain itself and developed considerable skill and considerable talent. In another the 'Profession' entertains the Army, as it has done so thoroughly since war began. Other aspects of the Army are shown in special Talks Department programmes, such as Radio Reconnaissance and War Commentary.

The BBC has a magnificent theme, and every department is trying to give to the public and to the Army itself at least an outline of the complex structure which is the modern British Army.

But during the planning and writing and rehearsing of this week, those responsible have kept clearly in mind not the Army as a whole but one man—the ordinary British Tommy, the man who in 1938 never dreamed of weapons and uniform, but who, in 1943, is at the lowest estimate, equal to the best fighting men of any other nation. It is to him we dedicate Army Week. To him we say: This is your story. This is your portrait. This is your life. We salute you and thank you. For we know that one day you will come home and say with inevitable casualness, 'Well, that's that. We've won.'

Radio Times October 8 1943 Vol. 81 No. 1045 Registered at the G.P.O. as a Newspaper

PRICE TWOPENCE

PROGRAMMES FOR
October 10—16

RADIO TIMES

JOURNAL OF THE BRITISH BROADCASTING CORPORATION

(INCORPORATING WORLD-RADIO)

BBC News Map No. 3

This map is specially drawn to help you in following BBC news bulletins. Cut it out and keep it by your set. The names on it will be used, as far as possible, in giving you the daily news from the Italian battle-front.

5, 1943 Vol. 78 No. 1014 Registered at the G.P.O. as a Newspaper

PROGRAMMES FOR
March 7—13

OPENCE

RADIO TIMES
JOURNAL OF THE BRITISH BROADCASTING CORPORATION
(INCORPORATING WORLD-RADIO)

BBC NEWS MAP

This map of the Russian battle-areas has been specially drawn to help you in following BBC news bulletins. Keep it near your set. So far as possible the names on it will be used as reference points in giving you the news from Russia. ● Towards the bottom right-hand corner Stalingrad marks the extreme eastern limit of the German advance immediately before the Russians, in November 1942, began their great offensive by storming the fortified line of the Middle Don. ● Maps of other war areas will be given from time to time.

BBC NEWS MAPS

In March 1943, *Radio Times* provided reference maps on the cover to enable listeners to keep abreast of news bulletins from the Eastern Front and from Tunisia. "Cut it out and keep it near your set," urged the cover line. In September (opposite page) a further map was published to help listeners track events following the Allied invasion of Italy.

Times, March 19, 1943 Vol. 78 No. 1016 Registered at the G.P.O. as a Newspaper

PROGRAMMES FOR
March 21—27

CE TWOPENCE

RADIO TIMES
JOURNAL OF THE BRITISH BROADCASTING CORPORATION
(INCORPORATING WORLD-RADIO)

BBC NEWS MAP No. 2—TUNISIA

This map is specially drawn to help you in following BBC news bulletins. Cut it out and keep it by your set. The names on it will be used, as far as possible, in giving you future news from Tunisia. BBC maps of other war areas will be printed as occasion arises.

Russia on the Map

'ALTOGETHER the Red Army have recaptured over 200 inhabited places, 35 of which are named in the communiqué.' So says the news-reader, and though even the 35 named places may not all be given in the BBC bulletin, listeners have been given what was more helpful, a clear general picture of each day's progress and its implications throughout the recent Russian offensive.

The staff of the Home News department work in two shifts of three days each. When the new shift comes on duty, the man in charge of the Russian story first takes a look at the large map of the battle-zone fixed to the wall of the news room, to see how the previous three days' fighting has gone. A network of differently coloured strings attached to pins shows the approximate battle-front for each day he has been off duty. Each night as the names of newly captured places come from Moscow, he puts in a new set of pins and connects them up in an outline of the new front. Then he tries to tell listeners what he sees, remembering always that most of them have nothing like so good a map, probably do not mark up what map they have, may not even be looking at one at all.

Radio Times (incorporating World-Radio) December 17 1943

Vol. 81 No. 1055 Registered at the G.P.O. as a Newspaper

PROGRAMMES FOR
December 19—25

PRICE TWOPENCE

RADIO ✶ TIMES
JOURNAL OF THE BRITISH BROADCASTING CORPORATION

'The Fifth Christmas'

Drawing by C. W. Bacon

CHRISTMAS 1943

As the war dragged on, an appropriately sombre Yuletide edition came with a cover illustration by Cecil W Bacon. The message of the centrepiece broadcast on Christmas Day (opposite) was: "We are advancing towards victory, towards understanding." Meanwhile, in the same issue *RT* reader Mrs E Holmes of Bradford wrote to complain about an episode of *Kitchen Front*, in which "a mere man" advised housewives on how to grill a steak. "We would be more grateful if we were told how to procure one," she said.

Full programmes for Christmas Week and Christmas Day

In this fifth year of war, and at the approach of its mighty climax, the simple symbols of Christmas and of the old ideals of peace and good-will need be none the less honoured because mankind has had to learn again that peace and goodwill must be fought for. BBC programmes during Christmas week will be found, as usual, to reflect the traditional spirit of the season, with a special thought this year for all whom the call of war has torn far from the homes they love and the kind of Christmas they like best to remember. To all in the fighting Services on Britain's battle-fronts, on land, in the air, and on the perilous seas; to the millions who toil with hand and brain in their staunch support; to all who now live in loneliness and anxiety—to all listeners, indeed, but this year to these in particular, 'Greetings!' And may you find among these programmes many happy memories of the past and a still happier promise for the future!

Here are pictures that will indicate something of the world-wide range of the big Christmas-afternoon broadcast. The programme will include contributions from (L. to R.) the Australian front in New Guinea ; the Italian front ; Chungking, war-ravaged but indomitable; and the great Alaskan Highway, 'built for war, ready for peace '.

'WE ARE ADVANCING'—the Christmas afternoon broadcast

Laurence Gilliam and Leonard Cottrell, producers of the world-wide Christmas-afternoon programme, describe the sweep of the ambitious radio journey planned by the BBC in co-operation with the General Post Office and the broadcasting organisations and fighting services of the United Nations

ON Christmas Day, the fifth of the war, the power of broadcasting is used to piece together for sixty brief minutes the pattern of a world torn asunder by war, to reveal something of the new pattern of unity towards which the peoples of the free world are struggling.

'We are Advancing, towards Victory, towards Understanding '—that is our theme this Christmas. Advancing on the battle-fronts, in Russia, in Italy, in the Pacific war-zones. Advancing in understanding as we work and fight together 'not for ourselves alone '.

A blending of sounds and voices brings a series of short pictures into focus as we move around the world.

First, a London home, where a soldier is spending his first Christmas at home for five years. He was a prisoner of war. Now he is home again. The walls dissolve, and we are in Italy, just behind the line of battle, with our fighting men. Our first greeting is to them in the name of all whose loved ones fight overseas.

* * * *

A voice without a name speaks next, telling of the dark hungry Christmas in the occupied lands. Then the bright cheerful noise of American airmen entertaining British fighter pilots 'somewhere in England '. Then a sharp reminder of the men who are on guard while you enjoy your Christmas. Over to Coastal Command, on patrol, guarding our ships. Then to the men who are building your ships—ships for the advance, to a Clyde shipyard for a greeting to all war-workers. Then to the Navy, at a North-Atlantic base. The men of the destroyers and the corvettes have a call to make across the Atlantic—over to Halifax, Nova Scotia, for a greeting to the Merchant Navy. Up North to Newfoundland to our first airman, a ferry pilot whose daily business it is to cross that same ocean in a few hours. We are advancing.

Across Canada to another war-time communication link, the Alaska Highway, built for war, ready for peace, the first stage of a new artery ready to bring new life to frozen lands. South, over the border to the Middle-West metropolis. From the skyscrapers of Chicago you cannot see the Atlantic or the Pacific. But some are beginning to see a new world. We are advancing.

Across the South Atlantic to Africa. A South African transport pilot speaks. He answers our greeting to the flying men who are cutting new swift lines across the dark continent, sends us back to Brazil, which joins our Christmas circle for the first time with a gay picture of Christmas in the sun. Now westward across the Pacific, south to New Guinea, to the bitter jungle. A heartfelt greeting to the fighting men advancing there, slowly, painfully, but still advancing.

North-west now to Chungking where another flying man broadcasts a message from war-torn China, great in hope and endurance. Westward again to India, where a British soldier from the Burma front sends greetings home on the eve of advance. Now the picture changes. From the scenes of war at sea, in the jungles, in the mountains and in the islands we pause at the home of peace. Across the world steals the sound of Christmas bells, bringing alive in countless hearts an old unredeemed promise of lasting peace. From the white hill-town of Bethlehem an ordinary soldier sends a message of hope to the world.

The sound of bells from the Holy Land will be echoed, we hope, by the sound of bells from one of the great cities of Russia. We shall greet our great Russian allies as they advance to complete the liberation of their land.

* * * *

Our journey nears its end. We are back in Britain in an ancient farmhouse in the Midlands. A farmer speaks to the world of the things that lie at the heart of all our lives, the land and the men who serve it.

Last scene of all : London—fighting men of many nations joined together to declare before the world their unity in the hard task that lies before them. The pledge is given. ' We are Advancing. Towards Victory. Towards Understanding.'

(L. to R.) From Rio de Janeiro will come a message from our ally, Brazil ; 'the men of the destroyers and corvettes' have a call to make across the Atlantic ; the bells of Bethlehem will renew their promise to mankind ; and from the English Midlands a farmer will speak of our own rich soil and the men who serve it

WITH THE BBC IN 1943

Mr. Fyodor Gusev, who became Russian Ambassador to Great Britain in August, broadcast a short message to this country on Russia's Day, November 7

Dr. T. V. Soong, Minister for Foreign Affairs in the Chinese Government, who visited Britain during the summer, broadcast the Sunday-night postscript on August 8

The death on August 26 of Professor John Hilton (left), whose weekly talks to the Forces were alive with sympathy and practical advice, and the death on November 20 of 'Romany' (seen here with 'Raq') deprived British radio of two striking personalities. Each of them had endeared himself to a wide listening public.

Leary N. Constantine, famous cricketer from Trinidad, now Welfare Officer for Jamaican technicians in England, broadcast a Friday night talk on September 3, and took part in the Brains Trust on May 23 and November 9

Françoise Rosay, celebrated French stage and screen actress, made her first appearance in British radio in the Anglo-French vaudeville programme on July 14, and broadcast the Sunday-night postscript on October 31, the anniversary of her escape from Marseilles in 1942. She has broadcast frequently to France from North Africa.

Lydia Lopokova was the woman narrator in the adaptation of Tolstoy's 'War and Peace', the broadcasting of which during January and February was an outstanding achievement in radio drama

Yehudi Menuhin, the famous American violinist, during a visit to this country broadcast with the BBC Symphony Orchestra in a concert at the Royal Albert Hall on April 5

Wynford Vaughan Thomas flew over Berlin in a Lancaster bomber on a September night raid, and recorded his impressions 'on the spot'

Howard Marshall, a popular BBC commentator on pre-war events, was with the first British troops to enter Tunis, and described the scene in a memorable despatch

The story of the making at Cwmgiedd of the film 'The Silent Village', based on the destruction of the Czech mining village of Lidice, was broadcast on June 10. Llew Jones, a miner, took part

'The Anvil', a series of programmes in January and February, dealt with listeners' questions on religious and ethical subjects. Here are (left to right) Canon F. A. Cockin, of St. Paul's Cathedral; Professor Victor Murray, University College, Hull, a Free Church layman (Methodist); and Father Agnellus Andrew, a Franciscan friar.

A scene at the Royal Albert Hall on August 21, the last night of the Promenade Concert season, when for the first time in the history of the Proms the BBC Symphony Orchestra and the London Philharmonic Orchestra were combined. Sir Henry Wood is seen shaking hands with Paul Beard (leader, BBC Symphony Orchestra) with Jean Pougnet (leader of the L.P.O.) on his left

'The Great Ship' made radio history, being performed three times in one week during May. Here John Gielgud (left) who played the principal part, and Eric Linklater (centre) the author, discuss the script with Val Gielgud, the producer, who is the BBC's Director of Features and Drama

A YEAR IN PICTURES

Their Majesties the King and Queen visited the Merchant Navy Club, London, on May 13. With them are shown (l. to r.) the Hon. John G. Winant, United States Ambassador to Great Britain; Howard Thomas, producer of 'Shipmates Ashore', the programme broadcast each week from the club; Major Laughton of the National Services Hostels Corporation; George Tomlinson, M.P., Parliamentary Secretary, Ministry of Labour; and (back to camera) Joe Loss, who provided music for the occasion.

BELOW : Some of the young refugees who took part in the Welsh Children's 'Goodwill Day' programme on May 18. Seated : Richard Mestitz (Czech); Judith and Frank Weisinger (Polish); standing, Lisette Delamoustier (Belgian)

ABOVE : Twice during the year Britain welcomed home repatriated prisoners-of-war—from Italy, on St. George's Day, and more recently from Germany. On each occasion recordings were made at the dockside and broadcast in BBC news bulletins.

Members of the Fourth Indian Contingent, during a visit to London, sent greetings to relatives and friends in India on September 10. Here I. B. Sarin of the BBC Indian Section introduces Subadar Lal Bahadur Thapa, V.C., from Nepal, to Princess Indira of Kapurthala, a regular broadcaster to India and to the Indian Forces

Since February the exchange series 'Transatlantic Call—People to People' has been broadcast jointly by the BBC and CBS of America. The Oldham spinners seen below typify the many ordinary folk who have spoken to their fellow-workers across the Atlantic.

The joyful note of Victory bells, from Westminster Abbey and elsewhere, was heard by listeners on two occasions during the year : May 16 (North Africa) and September 12 (Italy)

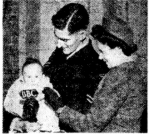

RIGHT : Perry John Batterham in the arms of his father, Corporal John Batterham of the Royal Australian Air Force, during his christening service, which was broadcast on September 28 in 'Anzacs Calling Home'. The producer, Flt. Lieut. H. H. Stewart, R.A.A.F., described this baby as 'the best baby and the worst broadcaster' he had ever met, for P. J. B. remained serenely silent throughout the ceremony.

ABOVE : A BBC recording truck as used in Italy and elsewhere by BBC war correspondents. Observer J. R. N. Nixon and (in the truck) Recording Engineer G. F. Wade are operating the recording equipment, which includes two hundred yards of microphone cable.

In July a broadcast commentary was given at a Naval Training Centre where submarine crews are taught to use the Davis Escape Apparatus. Gilbert Harding is shown talking to trainees about to take their first dip

L/Cpl. Jimmy Howe (right) with some members of the dance band he formed in Stalag VIII B. Most of them were repatriated in October. They broadcast on November 20.

Leslie Druett, Sussex farmer, talked to Joe Hayter, driver of a Lease-lend tractor, in a May broadcast of the series 'Transatlantic Call—People to People'

Some of the huge audience, mainly R.A.F. and W.A.A.F. of all ranks, who sat entranced by the playing of the BBC Symphony Orchestra, which visited their camp for concerts in September

HE MOMENT he has dreamed
rwhelming attack—is almos
ources of the whole country m
the fighting men—the ships a
ich normally distribute our c

Food **NF** Facts

ALL ABOUT THE NEW RATION BOOK

CUT THIS NOTICE OUT AND KEEP IT BY YOU

The issue of the new Ration Book (with the next Clothing Book) began on May 22nd. It will be used for food purchases from July 23rd.

Getting your new Ration Book will be easier and quicker this year if everyone follows these simple directions. We have divided them into BEFORE, DURING and AFTER. Take these stages one at a time, and you will help to make the job of giving out even 45,000,000 books go with a swing.

BEFORE — Before you can get your new Ration Book you must see that both your IDENTITY CARD and your PRESENT RATION BOOK are in order.

Your *Identity Card* should have been signed on the left-hand inside page. It should also have your present permanent address on it. If it has not, or if you have lost your card, go at once to your local National Registration Office (same address as the Food Office), taking your present Ration Book with you. Remember it's no good going to a ration book distribution centre if your Identity Card has been lost or is incorrect.

Page 3 of your PRESENT RATION BOOK has been left blank so far. This must be filled in now. *This page must not be cut out.* Next make sure that page 36 has the names and addresses of your retailers written or stamped in the spaces provided.

HOW TO GET THE NEW RATION BOOK

DURING — During the time that the new books are being given out, the posters in your Food Office area and advertisements in your local newspapers will tell you where and when to get your book. Remember that the poster to go by is the one in your own Food Office area. It will be shown in Post Offices, cinemas and elsewhere.

[...] your new Ration Book you must have your present Food [...] *Anyone can fetch your new book for you* [...] books for a household can [...]ent. Other arrangements [...]nd for their new book at

[...]ffice between now and July 23rd
[...]tion Books at the same time and
[...] Identity Cards who **have to**
[...] Books at the same time.

[...] Book you must :
[...]onal Registration Number on the
[...]ok and your name, address and
[...] on the front of the Clothing Book.

[...]ook carefully and put it away in a

MINISTRY OF FOOD

RATION BOOK

OFFICIAL PAID

HOLDER'S NAME AND REGISTERED ADDRESS

Compare with your Identity Card and report any difference to your Food Office

DO NOT ALTER

ISSUED

Surname WAKELING

Other Names

Address 5 Tillrow Cottages

Dawney.

High Wycombe Bucks.

W.I. FOOD FACTS No. 203

RADIO TIMES
JOURNAL OF THE BRITISH BROADCASTING CORPORATION
The war years 1944

ISSUED BY THE BOARD OF TRADE

Keep your clothes on their to save coupon

While they are new—

that's the time to take your clothes in hand if you want them to look well and last well. A few minutes 'maintenance' work early on will save hours of patching and renovating later. Here are a few suggestions from Make-do and Mend classes.

GET YOUR COPY *of the new " Make-do and Mend " illustrated booklet. It contains many useful hints on the care, mending and renovating of clothes and household linen. Obtainable from your bookseller or newsagent or H.M. Stationery Office. Price 3d.*

SEWING GOES WITH A SWING

at Make-do and Mend classes —and there's usually a machine you can use, and an iron for pressing. Your local Evening Institute, Technical College or Women's Organisation is probably running a class now. Or ask at the Citizens' Advice Bureaux—they'll give you particulars.

11 COUPONS PROTECTED
IF YOU CAN'T GET DRESS SHIELDS for your woollen frocks, make your own and proof them by soaking in an alum solution.

6 COUPONS AT STAKE
TO AVOID 'SEATING' SKIRT put in a half-lining of strong material—perhaps the bit of an old slip or lining. Make this a shade narrower than the back breadth so that it will reach from seam to seam at the back. It should come well over the hips.

8 COUPONS SAFEGUARDED
TO KEEP WOOLLIES IN GOOD SHAPE, stitch a tape along shoulder and underarm seams before the first wash and they won't sag.

ANOTHER COUPON-SAVER
ANCHOR ALL BUTTONS on children's clothes and your own woollies, by backing with a double band of material or tape.

AGAIN COUPON ECONOMY
STRENGTHEN STOCKINGS at the heels, toes and where your suspenders fasten, with bits of old stockings.

Home-made Handkerchiefs SAVE COUPONS
—make them from scraps of worn out sheets and pillowcases. Even old blouses and undies can be used, provided they are absorbent and will stand boiling.

Radio Times (incorporating World-Radio) — June 16 1944
Vol. 83 No. 1081 Registered at the G.P.O. as a Newspaper

PRICE TWOPENCE

PROGRAMMES FOR
June 18—

RADIO TIMES
JOURNAL OF THE BRITISH BROADCASTING CORPORATION

BBC at the Front

BBC war correspondents with the Navy, the Army, and the Air Force are with the fighting men on the Western Front, doing their biggest job of the war—collecting first-hand impressions and personal stories of the battle in Europe for broadcasting to listeners in Britain and, through the BBC's short-wave services, to the free world. Pictures of BBC war correspondents and the story of their activities are published on page 3

BBC mobile recording vans are overseas with the Allied armies; here a correspondent is seen recording his story from the roof of one of them

BBC war correspondents can record their stories and the sounds of battle in areas where it would be impossible to take their trucks. Some of them carry a compact recording unit little bigger than a portable gramophone

A.E.F. Programme
On the morning of June 7— the day after D-Day—the BBC began broadcasting to Western Front Forces the Allied Expeditionary Forces Programme, which it has undertaken in agreement with Supreme Headquarters. The daily programmes include contributions from the existing programmes of the BBC, the American Forces Network, and the Canadian Broadcasting Corporation. The new programme is broadcast from 5.55 a.m. to 11 p.m. D.B.S.T on a wavelength of 285 metres, 1050 kilocycles per second.

G.B.S.
'Starred' Programme
Bernard Shaw's *The Adventures of the Black Girl in her Search for God*, adapted as a radio play, is Monday night's 'starred' programme—the BBC's choice for the week. The part of the Black Girl is played by Elisabeth Welch, and others in the strong cast include Hubert Gregg, Leslie Perrins, Malcolm Graeme, and Julian Mitchell. Lionel Hale, dramatic critic, introduces the programme in an article on page 5.

General Booth Centenary
General Carpenter, head of the Salvation Army, will give the address at Sunday evening's service, which will mark the centenary of William Booth's conversion. It will be broadcast from the Booth Memorial Hall in Nottingham, built to honour the founder of the Salvation Army by his fellow citizens. From this Sunday the evening service begins at 7.45, not 8 o'clock.

'Framley Parsonage'
This story, the fourth of Anthony Trollope's novels with the Barsetshire setting, has been adapted as a twelve-part radio serial for broadcasting on Sunday evenings between 8.30 and 9. The first part will be broadcast next Sunday. The novel first appeared as a serial in the *Cornhill Magazine* in 1861. Its action is principally in East Barset where Mark Roberts, the young vicar of Framley, finds himself involved in the 'power politics' of the county. Listeners who enjoyed *The Warden* will meet several old acquaintances, among them Bishop Proudie and his redoubtable lady.

April Appeals
The following are the results to date of the Week's Good Cause appeals broadcast in April. Co-operative Youth Movement National Federation of Young Farmers' Clubs, by the Rt. Hon. A. V. Alexander, C.H., M.P., £1,002 17s. 4d. ; St. Mary's Hospitals for Women and Children, Manchester, by Wing Commander Guy Gibson, V.C., £2,702 17s. 0d. ; National Y.M.C.A. War Service Fund, by Sir Frank Newson-Smith, £7,594 2s. 6d.; British Empire Leprosy Relief Association, by 'Leprosy Doctor,' £7,238 11s. 2d. ; Old People's Welfare Committee of the National Council of Social Service, by the Rt. Hon. Margaret Bondfield, £3,404 0s. 0d.

'Alexander Nevsky'
On Thursday, the third anniversary of the German invasion of Russia, there will be a repeat of this radio play based on Eisenstein's film with its music by Prokofiev. Alexander Nevsky, Russian hero, led the army that defeated the Teutonic Knights on the ice of Lake Peipus in 1242.

Sportsmen's Corner
On Wednesday evening Harold Abrahams, the Cambridge athlete who won the 100-metre race for Britain at the 1924 Paris Olympic Games, will discuss outstanding events of Olympic Games meetings with Willy Meisl, Viennese athlete, international footballer and swimmer, and writer on European sport who is now serving in the British Army.

Saturday's 'Stalin' Mile
Harold Abrahams is also giving the commentary on this short-limit handicap to be run at the Manchester Athletic Ground, Fallowfield. The event was christened by Fred Williams, Secretary of the Manchester Athletic Club, who the proceeds of the athletic meeting in 1943 went, as they will go again this year, to Mrs. Churchill's Aid-to-Russia Fund.

Saturday-Night Theatre
This week listeners can hear *The Lilies of the Field*, a comedy by John Hastings Turner, first produced at the Ambassador's Theatre, London, in 1923.

Printed in England by WATERLOW & SONS, LTD., Twyford Abbey Road, Park Royal, N.W.10, and Scarle Road, Wembley, Middlesex.

Richard Dimbleby—with the R.A.F. First BBC war correspondent, serving in France in 1939, then in the Middle East. First BBC observer to fly to Berlin on a night bombing raid

Guy Byam, jumped with first paratroops on D-Day—his ninth jump. He was an R.N.V.R. officer in the Navy and Combined Operations until wounded and invalided out of the Service

Frank Gillard—with the Army. The only BBC reporter in the Dieppe raid, August 1942. Then to the Middle East and the Eighth Army, serving from Mareth to Cassino

D-DAY AND BEYOND
Just days after the Normandy invasion on Friday 6 June, *Radio Times* explained on its cover and on page 3 how the BBC's reporters and technical experts in its War Reporting Unit would bring listeners the latest news of the war on land, sea and air.

June 6 . . . the assault on the beaches of Northern France

'A Great Responsibility'

The BBC's War Reporting Unit came into full action on D-Day, June 6. Here you can read of the vital task it has set out to do and how it hopes to accomplish it

GENERAL EISENHOWER'S signal for the opening of the Western Front did more than despatch great armadas of ships and men, guns, tanks, and aeroplanes across the Channel to the beaches of France. It set thumping the hearts of people everywhere : people whose fathers, husbands, and sons are serving in the Allied armies ; and those to whom the signal meant still greater effort at work to keep the armies supplied.

The King, broadcasting on June 6, called his people to prayer : 'We who remain in this land can most effectively enter into the sufferings of subjugated Europe by prayer, whereby we can fortify the determination of our sailors, soldiers, and airmen, who go forth to set the captives free.'

To the BBC it gave an added responsibility : people at home and overseas would want and would expect a comprehensive service of news and commentary from the battlefields across the English Channel.

* * *

D-Day brought the BBC face to face with one of its biggest tasks in this war : to keep listeners informed of the progress of the Allied armies, to take its microphones to the beaches and battlefields, into the air, to bring to listeners at home, by personal stories as well as by official communiqués, the story of the assault and of the deeds of the men taking part in it.

With weeks of painstaking preparation behind it, the BBC War Reporting Unit, already actively engaged on the Italian and Far Eastern battlefronts, went into action with the Allied Forces. Within a few hours listeners were hearing accounts of the landings from men who themselves had landed on the beaches and had flown over them.

BBC war correspondents are accredited to land, sea, and air forces, and each one of them has shared in the rigorous routine training of the particular unit whose activities he is now reporting. They face the same dangers as the fighting men, and their job is to collect complete and accurate pictures of the assault as it develops.

Correspondents with the first troops to land in France took portable recording equipment with them—each unit little bigger than a portable gramophone. In time, mobile recording trucks will be used in France as they have been used in North Africa and Italy, and eventually mobile transmitters will be set up in liberated territories.

But at the moment, getting the stories on the spot is a difficult enough job ; getting them back to BBC headquarters is another job—and was not the least exciting for those correspondents who went with the invading forces. Howard Marshall, correspondent with the land forces, was twice in the sea during his adventurous return to Britain on D-Day evening : water dripped from his sodden uniform as he recorded his account of the scenes on the landing beaches.

The BBC team of correspondents with the ground forces already includes Colin Wills, Frank Gillard, Pierre Lefêvre, Guy Byam, Robert Barr, and Chester Wilmot. Others will join them later. Byam went into action with the British parachutists and Wilmot with the glider-borne forces.

The naval team is headed by Michael Standing and includes A. C. Fletcher, Richard North, and Stanley Maxted. David Bernard is BBC

Howard Marshall, BBC Director of War Reporting, with the Army. Well known for his peacetime commentaries on cricket and boxing. After three years as Public Relations Director of Ministry of Food, rejoined BBC last year as war correspondent for the North African campaign

Michael Standing—with the Navy. An experienced commentator, he has been with BBC Outside Broadcasting department since 1936

H. O. Sampson—engineer with the Army. . . . Much responsibility rests with these men who are not in the limelight of publicity: they are in charge of recording and transmitting equipment

Photographs of other members of the War Reporting Unit will be published in following issues of 'Radio Times'

correspondent with the Merchant Navy. Richard Dimbleby, Stewart McPherson, and Kent Stevenson report the war in the air, with Colston Shepherd supplying the strategic picture in the rear. Reporting the activities of the American Forces are Robert Dunnet and Robin Duff. The Americans also have their own radio correspondents in the field, and BBC technical facilities have been placed at their disposal where necessary.

Vital links in the chain between correspondents at the Front and the listener at home are the BBC engineers in charge of the recording and transmitting equipment. Then there is the Traffic Control Unit which must ensure that the messages of war correspondents are cleared expeditiously through the normal news and censorship channels.

Many difficulties, technical and administrative, had to be overcome in the months of preparation for D-Day, but those responsible must have felt amply repaid when at H-Hour the BBC War Reporting Unit went into action as planned.

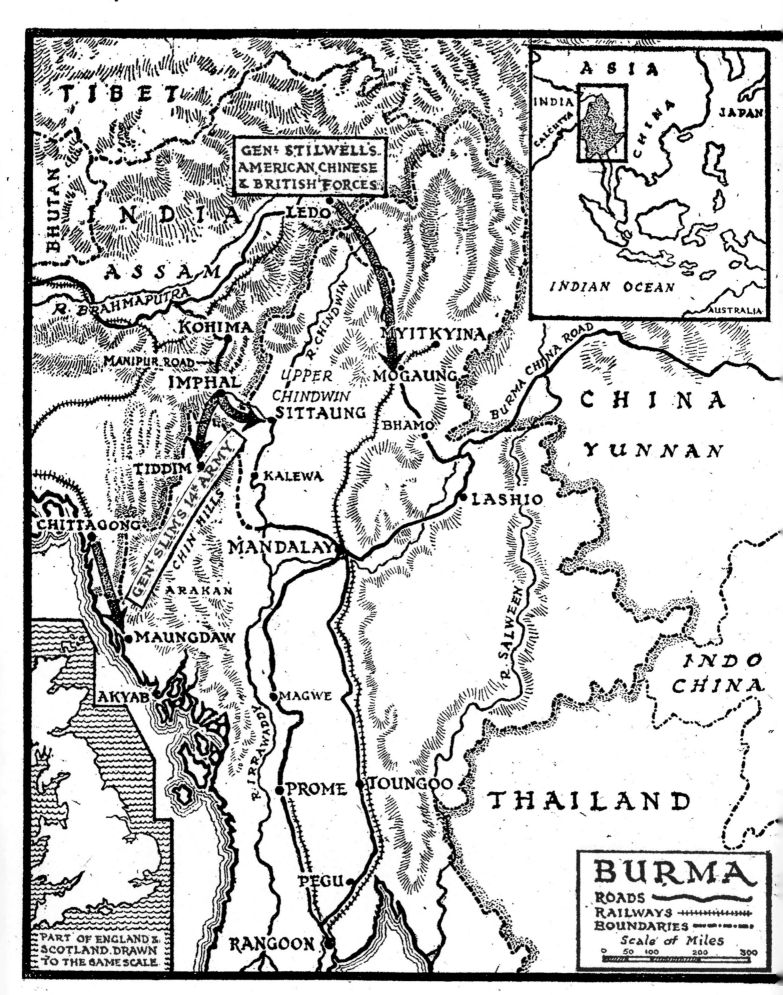

GEN! STILWELL'S AMERICAN, CHINESE & BRITISH FORCES

GEN! SLIM'S 14th ARMY

BURMA

ROADS ━━━━━━
RAILWAYS ┼┼┼┼┼┼┼
BOUNDARIES ━·━·━·━
Scale of Miles
0   50   100   200   300

PART OF ENGLAND & SCOTLAND DRAWN TO THE SAME SCALE

Mother's time off

RAILWAYS AT WAR

The words of the warm tribute recently paid to the railways of Britain by the Prime Minister glow proudly from the notice-boards of every station. All that the railways continually do to justify that tribute becomes increasingly obvious with

every week of war. It would be mere impudence for us to enlarge here upon the terrific tasks they are undertaking and the still greater burden everybody expects to be placed upon their capable shoulders in the near future. Sufficient for us to point out that the BBC's biggest tribute so far to the war-time work of the railways will be paid on March 24 in the form of a special programme. The producer, Cecil McGivern, proposes to 'build' an imaginary but representative railway junction complete with station, divisional offices, marshalling yard, locomotive works, and so on. His half-hour programme will cover twelve hours of work at this junction: and various flash-backs and side-glances will record previous incidents in the complex and diversified tale of the junction's war-work.

5 lbs. OF COAL SAVED IN ONE DAY BY 40,000 HOMES WILL [ENO]UGH FUEL TO [CH]URCHILL TANK

...al are used in 2 hours by ... or electric oven.

WAR IN THE EAST

Keeping up with news of the Battle for Burma was difficult. This extract (below) from a letter from BBC correspondent Richard Sharp was dated 27 February and appeared in the issue of *RT* dated 26 May...

BBC War Correspondent on Burma Front

These extracts are from a letter written on February 27 by Richard Sharp, BBC Correspondent in the South-East Asia Command, describing how he got into the Seventh Division Box on the Arakan front and how he got his stories back

I ARRIVED in this transit camp last evening, a dusty and, I fear, unsoldierly spectacle, wearing a bush shirt which would not button, filthy [co]tton trousers, once green, tied up with a piece of [ba]ndage, and brown gym shoes. I had my type-[w]riter, sleeping bag, and shaving stuff in a pack, [a]nd was slung about with binoculars and water-[bo]ttle. . . . I had made up my mind that the eastern [en]d of the Seventh Division Box would be opened [fi]rst, not the Ngakyedauk end. So I walked over [th]e Goppe, with my gear on a mule, and begged [m]y way by horse and foot down to where we were [t]rying to fight a way in. For two days I sat on [a] grilling O.P. and watched men trying to take [s]ome brown pimples across the paddy fields. Then [a] man mentioned that tanks could come in and get [o]ut of the box, so I cadged a lift in one. " Here [I] am," I thought, " the first reporter in this box." And then someone said : " The Ngakyedauk was [o]pened today, and another correspondent came in

two hours ago." I had left him in a camp a week back. All that week he had sat there peacefully waiting, and then got in and out with the first convoy. He guessed better than I did. I sent four or five despatches while tramping. Sending each separate one was a separate achievement. One would hear of a mule train or a liaison officer or a despatch walker, and entrust it to him under oath. . . . I actually started to walk back over the Goppe with one, seven miles there and seven back, when a swift-marching man caught up with me and took it with him.

' I stayed in the box two nights and was uplifted. These men are a steady lot. . . . Yesterday I had arranged to go out the eastern way again, and go on watching the fight. A Bren carrier was to be the vehicle. But I met two Public Relations photographers and came out over the Ngakyedauk instead. A grand feeling now, to have on clean clothes and be washed all over.'

The BBC has two war correspondents on the Burma Front, John Nixon and Richard Sharp. This photograph of Sharp was taken when he was with the Seventh Indian Division

Radio Times (incorporating World-Radio)   June 30 1944
Vol. 84 No. 1083 Registered at the G.P.O. as a Newspaper

PRICE TWOPENCE

RADIO ✤ TIMES
JOURNAL OF THE BRITISH BROADCASTING CORPORATION

'Spirit of '76'
Tuesday is American Independence Day, and for the occasion D. G. Bridson has written this special programme which will be broadcast after the 9 o'clock News. It will tell the story of a group of American soldiers serving in the early stages of the War of Independence. The narration is cast in romantic ballad form, and special music for choir and orchestra is based on American fighting songs. Music specially written for the occasion by William Alwyn will be played by a section of the London Symphony Orchestra, conducted by Muir Mathieson.

U.S.A. Army Band
The United States Army Band, now in Britain to entertain Allied invasion forces at the request of General Eisenhower, is playing twice—in the Home Service and GFP—on Tuesday evening. The eighty-six-piece band is under the direction of Captain Thomas F. Darcy, jnr., one of America's foremost band-music composers. Included within its organisation is a nineteen-piece dance band.

Facing Suffering
The first of three talks by people who have faced suffering and bereavement, and found victory over them in Christian Faith, will be broadcast on Wednesday evening at 7.40 in the Home Service. The speaker will be a man badly wounded in the last war.

Services for Isolated Units
During July the Rev. Pat Leonard, known to British troops throughout the world for his work with Toc H and as Boy Scout leader, is to conduct the 10.15 Sunday-morning service in the G.F.P. These services are planned especially for men serving in outlandish places who have no padre of their own and cannot get to a church.

Sportsmen's Corner
In Wednesday evening's G.F.P. review, outstanding events in the history of the Manchester Athletic Club will be recalled by W. M. Donaldson and Fred T. Williams in a chat with Henry Rose. And in an interview with Captain G. H. Troughton, R. W. Armstrong will speak from his experience of 'Sixty-eight Years of Racing.'

Commander, R.N.
On the bridge of one of H.M. ships today a Commander, R.N., walks backwards and forwards . . . he began his career as a cadet at Dartmouth and served in the last war. After 1918 he found himself 'passed over' for the coveted brass hat, and eventually was retired. When this war came, he was recalled and at last came into his own. That is the theme of Friday night's Home Service programme, which shows the hardships and highlights of a Naval career. The author is Commander Gilbert Hackforth-Jones.

Wilfred in Westmorland
On Sunday, in the Children's Hour, Wilfred Pickles visits Westmorland markets and horse fairs and village festivals, learning about the everyday life and work of the county. The names of his points of call are sure to revive holiday memories in many listeners.

FALL OF ROME

BBC correspondent Godfrey Talbot featured on the cover of this July edition capturing the mood of the crowd on the Via del Impero in central Rome as the Allies took control of the city on 5 June.

OPPOSITE a feature outlines just how important music was to RAF pilots and aircrew who were often stationed in isolated places and therefore "cut off from public cinema, theatres and dances".

'There never was such a Roman holiday'

June 5, 1944. . . . Godfrey Talbot, BBC war correspondent, broadcasting from liberated Rome to the people of Britain from the Via Del Impero, the place where Mussolini declared war on the Allies. His broadcast is one of the most memorable of the war. . . .' There never was such a Roman holiday. The capital is going wild and people are shouting: "Oh, we have been waiting for you so long. Thank God you've come at last"'

Meet the BBC's War Correspondents

Chester Wilmot, Australian with the Army. Covered first Libyan campaign, and was in Greece, Tobruk, and New Guinea for A.B.C.

Robert Barr. Came to the BBC from 'Daily Mail' in August 1941. Particularly associated with the BBC feature, 'Marching On'

News of the G.F.P.
It is always a complicated job planning a radio service because different listeners want their pet programmes at different hours of the day. It is ten times more difficult planning General Forces Programme because there are at least ten different groups of listeners stretching from the Burma Front to West Africa. Even the old rule that most people listen between 7 and 10.30 p.m. does not apply to G.F.P. On the Burma Front, for example, all radio is turned off from dusk to dawn so that inquisitive Jap patrols cannot take their bearings by keeping their ears skinned for the voice of Vera Lynn or the strains of 'Lillibulero' before the news bulletins.

*   *   *

And this is part of a letter to Joan Griffiths : 'After reading several letters and an article in a newspaper recently received from those fair shores, in which much criticism is levelled at the G.F.P. . . . Well we like it, nay we think it "Just the job." Forgive mistakes, but Spike Hughes is on the air at the moment. One of the suggestions of my pal was that perhaps on one of your talks you could dwell upon lush dewy green grass, as he is "cheesed" with this dusty white bone-dry sand.'

The Royal Air Force believes in music as recreation for its flying and ground personnel serving at home and overseas. Next Monday, after the 9 o'clock News, you can hear in one programme four of its star performers, the Central Band, the Symphony Orchestra, the Dance Orchestra, and the Griller Quartet. Here an R.A.F. Officer describes the organisation which ensures that . . .

R.A.F. Men are Never Music-hungry

MUSIC has always been regarded by the Directorate of Air Force Welfare as one of its most important activities. Every effort has been made not only to encourage talented performers, but to enable them to play to the largest possible Service audiences.

Air Commodore S. Graham, M.C., G.M., who last autumn succeeded Air Commodore H. Peake as Director of Welfare, has steadfastly pursued this policy and given the fullest scope and collaboration to the organising ability of Wing Commander R. P. O'Donnell, M.V.O., the R.A.F.'s well-known Director of Music.

Here very briefly is an outline of the organisation that brings Bach, Sousa, and the best swing to R.A.F. men serving in all theatres of war.

First there is the famous Central Band of eighty musicians, which, as old listeners will recall, was formed in 1920 by Flight Lieutenant J. H. Amers, M.B.E. He was the R.A.F.'s first Director of Music. Music for all official ceremonial occasions connected with the R.A.F. is provided by the Central Band, but since the war it has frequently been divided into two sections to meet all the many calls made upon it.

The Royal Air Force Symphony Orchestra, which is conducted by Wing Commander R. P. O'Donnell, is forty strong and was formed about three years ago. Its members include many leading chamber-music players and some of the finest instrumentalists from leading symphony orchestras. The string section is outstanding in English music, for it includes the entire personnel of the Griller, Blech, and Hirsch Quartets and of the Grinke Trio. The woodwind and brass sections, too, have their fair share of celebrities : Rowland Dyson, principal trumpet, was formerly with the London Philharmonic Orchestra ; Richard Walthew was principal clarinet of the BBC Midland Orchestra ; Cecil James comes from the London Symphony Orchestra, where he played principal bassoon ; and Dennis Brain, principal horn, is the son of Aubrey Brain of the BBC Symphony Orchestra. Many more players of distinction have been gathered together by

Wing Commander O'Donnell, among them Denis Matthews, who at the age of twenty-two is regarded as one of our foremost pianists.

Then there is the fourteen-piece Royal Air Force Dance Orchestra. Like the Symphony Orchestra, it has done great work in entertaining factories throughout the country engaged in aircraft production, in addition to broadcasting and its official duties. Comment on its high standard is not surprising, for its players were star men in the orchestras of Ambrose, Eddie Carroll, Lew Stone, Brian Lawrance, Oscar Rabin, Jack Hylton, and Jack Harris before the war.

The fourth of the R.A.F. musical units is the internationally famous Griller String Quartet, which provides special programmes of chamber music for the considerable number of R.A.F. men with a preference for this music.

All four Units come under the control of Wing Commander O'Donnell, who, incidentally, can claim the distinction of being the only Director of Music who has served in all three Services.

As listeners know, these four units by no means represent the sum-total of music that the R.A.F. can provide. The bands of the five

Wing Commander O'Donnell, Director of Music of the R.A.F., with Frederick Grinke, the well-known violinist and leader of the R.A.F. Symphony Orchestra

A seven-piece R.A.F. Command dance band playing at a Spitfire Wing of the Desert Air Force in Italy.

Commands — Coastal, Bomber, Fighter, Technical, and Flying Training—have broadcast many times.

Then there is the imposing total of 109 five-piece R.A.F. dance bands attached to stations —often in remote places, such as the Orkneys, Shetlands, and Hebrides—where normal entertainment simply does not exist. Most of these bands are playing in the United Kingdom, but some are in East Africa, in Aden, in the Azores, Iceland, and Gibraltar, South Africa and West Africa. Ten of them have been touring the Middle East, sharing the discomforts of campaign life in common with other R.A.F. men. They played in the African desert ; they played at the Anzio beachhead, and are now with the troops in Italy. The Directorate of Air Force Welfare relies on these overseas dance bands to keep the men cheerful and happy.

Being an R.A.F. dance bandsman in the United Kingdom is not a whole-time job, because as well as providing music and entertainment where it is most needed, the men have to spend half their time on General Duties, doing routine jobs in the same way as other serving men.

The credit for starting these dance bands— mostly five-piece—belongs to the late Sir Walford Davies, who suggested the idea in 1940.

That, in hard fact, is a brief outline of the organisation that the R.A.F. has brought into being to entertain its men. From some quarters there has been criticism of the lavishness of it all, but undeserved when one remembers that R.A.F. flying men and ground crews are mostly static units, stationed miles away on isolated moors, in the wilds of Scotland, on the plains of England, behind as well as on the battlefronts, cut off from public cinemas, theatres and dances. The R.A.F. faced with the job of brightening the routine life of static bases—has succeeded.

This is the Royal Air Force Dance Band : its players include star men from the peacetime orchestras of Ambrose, Eddie Carroll, Lew Stone, Brian Lawrance, Oscar Rabin, Jack Hylton, and Jack Harris
(This picture, a still from the unreleased Vera Lynn film One Exciting Night, *is reproduced by courtesy of Columbia Pictures)*

Radio Times (incorporating World-Radio) December 22, 1944
Vol. 86 No. 1108 Registered at the G.P.O. as a Newspaper

RADIO TIMES

2D

BBC PROGRAMMES

Christmas Eve to December 30

H.M. THE KING WILL BROADCAST ON CHRISTMAS DAY AT 3 P.M.

☆

'The Journey Home'
Sixth Christmas radio journey of the war

☆

Services from Norwich and Southwark Cathedrals,
Ampleforth Abbey, Cransley Parish Church, and
St. Peter's, Harrogate

☆

Carol Services from Field-Marshal Montgomery's
Headquarters in the Field and from King's College
Chapel, Cambridge

☆

'Christmas Night at Eight,' with Arthur Askey, Gert
and Daisy, and Barbara Mullen

☆

Jack Buchanan tells the story of 'Sunny'

☆

'In Town Tonight'—301st edition

☆

Handel's oratorio, 'Messiah,' with the Huddersfield
Choral Society

Low on Laughter   ☆   Handley in 'Itma'
Ralph Richardson in Shakespeare's 'King John'

☆

Sir Cedric Hardwicke and Vic Oliver in 'The Big Show'

☆

The British, American, and Canadian Bands of the A.E.F.

☆

Charles Dickens's 'The Chimes'
Pantomimes   ☆   Music-Hall

Modern and Old-Time
Dance Music

A TIME OF HOPE

"This is the sixth Christmas of war," wrote Archbishop of York Cyril Garbett in a letter to readers, but amid the weariness there was optimism that the end was perhaps in sight and at last the country could begin to contemplate "the Journey Home".

RADIO TIMES

...ATED DECEMBER 22, 1944

The Good News of Christmas

A message from the Archbishop of York

...HIS is the sixth Christmas of war. But it will be happier for most of us than the preceding five. The danger of invasion has passed, ...nd the worst of the air raids are over. With quiet confidence we ...e end in sight. We hope that by next Christmas some of those ...bsent from us will have returned to their homes. And though we ...that there will be a hard struggle both in Europe and in the Far ...before victory is won, we begin to plan and to look forward to a new ...etter world.

...e experience of the last thirty years will have taught nothing unless ...s convinced all thoughtful men and women that a new world can ...eated neither by science nor by force. Science and force may be ...either for good or for evil. Man's greatest discoveries may make for ...ress or destruction. Their right use depends on the kind of man ...possesses them. We have created a new material world, but we ...not yet created the man who can be trusted to use wisely the ...zing inventions which science places in his hands.

... once again many are asking if outside themselves there is creative ...er which will change human nature. At Christmas the Church ...vers by pointing to a new-born infant, lying in a straw-lined manger ...dst the sheep and oxen under a rough shelter in the small city of ...hlehem. It asserts that through the birth, life, death and resurrection ...that child there came into the world a new power which would ...sform human character.

...nd the new power was not a philosophy or an impersonal force, but ...Son of the Eternal God, who by His Spirit is able to enter into the ...s of all who find room for Him and who will make them like Himself ...ove and self-sacrifice.

...hristmas therefore commemorates two stupendous facts. First that ...d in His love did actually send His Son into the world at a definite ...torical date. Notice how definite the Gospel is about dates and places : ...tates that Jesus was born in Bethlehem in Judah when Augustus was ...peror and Cyrenius was Governor. This preciseness about dates is

meant to make it clear that the birth of Christ is not a fairy story belonging to a dim 'once upon a time,' but an actual event which took place in human history. And secondly that He who was born in Bethlehem through His Spirit offers power to all who believe in Him to become true sons of God. It is this faith in power from above which saves the Christian from disillusionment and pessimism and enables him to look forward with hope to a new order in which men will use rightly and unselfishly all the gifts which modern science offers.

This is the message of God's love, and of hope for the future, which on Christmas Day will be proclaimed in all our churches. And to those who do not enter the churches the bells will ring out the good tidings. But it will also be heard by millions who are far away from churches and their bells; for the wireless will carry the news to lonely farms, to shepherds watching their flocks in distant glens, to sailors crossing the seas, and to millions who in Europe and Asia are offering their lives for the freedom of mankind.

Broadcasting is one of the great modern inventions which can be used either for the blessing or for the degradation of mankind. It serves as the channel through which either goodness, truth and beauty, or hate, fear and lying propaganda can be poured into the minds of multitudes. At its best it helps men to love God and their fellows; while at its worst it exploits their ignorance, and inflames bitterness and suspicion between nations as well as between individuals. As in the first century the Roman roads and the Greek language were instruments for the spread of the Gospel, so in the twentieth century the wireless and the English tongue are means by which God's message of love and peace can spread throughout the world. From early morning to late at night on Christmas Day the wireless will carry both to those at home and to their friends and kinsfolk far away the good news of God's love to mankind and His promise of peace to men of good will.

Cyril Ebor:

'The Journey Home'

An introduction to the world-wide Christmas afternoon programme, the sixth wartime radio journey

...OR five Christmases since war began radio reunions have linked our people at home, our fighting men, our kinsmen and our Allies ...

Scotland the voice of a soldier on Christmas leave, happy forerunner of many men under arms, sends a cheerful greeting to his less fortunate comrades. From Northern Ireland comes a greeting to all ...

at which partisans, who have fought underground for their right to live as free men in their own city again, are entertaining some of their countrymen who have been broadcasting to them from London throughout the occupation. On to Holland, a sad and bitter Christmas scene, and to Belgium with

1945

ANTARCTIC EXPEDITION

In March 1945, a hero of the past was honoured on the cover of *Radio Times* and in an article inside (opposite page) when the Home Service broadcast a dramatised account of Sir Ernest Shackleton's 1914–16 expedition aboard the *Endurance*.

Every schoolboy longs to be an explorer, and we are all schoolboys at heart.   That is why true stories of exploration have a universal appeal.   We know you will enjoy listening to Monday's programme at 9.30 p.m., a dramatised tale of Sir Ernest Shackleton's 1914-1916 Antarctic Expedition

South with Shackleton

By Squadron-Leader L. D. A. HUSSEY, R.A.F.,
a member of Sir Ernest Shackleton's last two Polar Expeditions who is taking part in Monday evening's broadcast

Aboard Shackleton's 'Endurance' locked fast in the Antarctic ice

IT was typical of Shackleton that he named his ship *Endurance*. He himself was never driven from his course by disappointments—and he had plenty of them. His expedition of 1914-1916 was, in a way, a failure—but one of the most brilliant failures in history. We set off in our little wooden sailing ship, *Endurance*, just before the first world war broke over Europe. We placed the ship and ourselves at the immediate disposal of the authorities, but were ordered by H.M. King George V and by the Admiralty to proceed. Incidentally, we had on board a Union Jack presented to us by the King. We were as well equipped as science could make us in those days. Radio was in its infancy, and we had only one small receiving set which, we were told, might receive up to a hundred miles. A radio transmitter of those days was much too heavy and cumbersome to take on the expedition.

We sailed south, calling at South America on the way, and penetrated the ice into regions hitherto unseen by man, discovering two hundred miles of new coastline and new ranges of mountains.

Then the worst winter for many generations took us in its grip. The sea froze to a depth of between sixty and eighty feet, and we froze in with it. For months we drifted helplessly, locked fast in the ice. Occasionally a seal would make a welcome addition to our larder, and we kept scurvy, that most dreaded Polar sickness, at bay with a ration of one raw potato each a week.

The dramatic events of that time will be reconstructed in the programme. For six months after we lost the ship we drifted over the sea on a piece of ice—day and night, at the mercy of the elements. At times our piece of ice was large enough to allow us to take a certain amount of exercise, but later under the currents and the swell it broke up and became so small until it would hardly accommodate us all.

All of us were tired, hungry, and very thirsty at times, but in this ordeal Shackleton was at his best. We were walking round our little piece of ice one day when he said to me: 'Huss! When the old mark goes to ground, a new one must be set up. Now I've got to see all you through this safely.'

Once, when things looked particularly hopeless, he and I dressed up in some old rags of uniform and, with a piece of string round our waists, from which dangled a spade for a sword, we solemnly inspected the camp.

Going to bed on our ice-floe was a simple job. We took off our boots, put them under our heads for a pillow, and climbed into our cocoon-like fur sleeping bags fully dressed. Morning found us lying in a pool of melted ice, thawed by the warmth of our bodies. I have slept on the sand of the Sudan, out on the frozen lava fields of Iceland, and in the snow-covered forests of Russia, but for sheer comfort give me a large slab of ice. Sand is hard and rocks, even frozen ones, have uncomfortable projections; but sea ice melts just where you curve in and out, and fits your body better than any feather mattress.

In the end our piece of ice became so small that we had to take to the boats—the small ship's lifeboats that we had kept with us and had dragged from one icy home to another. In our little open boats we spent six of the worst days and nights that I have ever known—cold, hungry, frost-bitten, and drifting over the freezing sea.

Eventually we landed on Elephant Island, uninhabited and snow-covered, where twenty-two of us lived for four and a half months under primitive conditions. You may remember my telling you about our life on Elephant Island in a *Travellers' Tales* broadcast some time ago, but Monday's programme will cover a far wider canvas: in fact the whole

Squadron-Leader L. D. A. Hussey, R.A.F.

story of the Shackleton Expedition, the voyage out, the wreck, and the rescue. You will hear of the boat journey that Shackleton made to get help for us—one of the greatest boat journeys in history. With five companions he fought his way through the worst seas in the world, in storms such as he had never before experienced during his thirty years at sea, storms in which well-found ships were lost with all hands. The actual boat is now in the grounds of Dulwich College—Shackleton's old school. But of its heroic crew not one is alive today. In the broadcast their places will be taken by men whose voices and accents approximate as nearly as possible to the originals, and the words that they will use are those which were actually spoken during those long, weary, cheerless and comfortless days when they were so close to death.

How they won through and rescued us all makes a tale as thrilling as any that has been written. In fact, when we who are left look back upon it we can hardly believe that we could have gone through it all and have survived. We have few material possessions to stir up our memories: I have one, an old banjo, which I treasure. Cannibals have listened in silence to its music in the heart of Africa. It was our only source of amusement during the long Polar night when we drifted, frozen in, for fifteen hundred miles. The last thing saved from our ship, almost as she sank, was this banjo. Sir Ernest jumped aboard and rescued it, saying: 'We must save that banjo, it's vital mental medicine.' He said afterwards that the banjo was one of the greatest factors in getting us all through alive and well. It went through the last war with me, narrowly escaping destruction more than once. It came south with us again on our last expedition in the *Quest* in 1921, when Scout Marr accompanied us—he is now back in the Antarctic in the research ship *Discovery*.

I played some of the old tunes on it to Sir Ernest the night he died. He said: 'I love those tunes, Huss. They make me feel sad or cheerful, just as I wish. And they help me forget my troubles.' You will hear them, too, on that same banjo.

I think this programme will give you an insight into the human side of Sir Ernest's character. He was really born four hundred years too late. He would have made a fitting companion for Raleigh, Hawkins, and Drake. A sailor to his finger tips, he had that streak of poetry in him that comes from spending long night watches alone on the bridge. His memory was astounding, and he was always ready with an apt quotation, often from some obscure poet. Browning was his favourite, and his favourite lines were: 'Ah, that a man's reach should exceed his grasp, or what's a Heaven for?' That sums him up—never satisfied, always striving to get further and to reach higher; not for any selfish ends, but for the sheer joy of finding out.

Radio Times (incorporating World-Radio)   May 10, 1945
Vol. 87 No. 1128 Registered at the G.P.O. as a Newspaper

RADIO TIMES

2d

BBC Victory Programmes

THURSDAY, MAY 10, to FRIDAY, MAY 18, inclusive

National Thanksgiving Service from St. Paul's Cathedral

☆

Mr. Churchill broadcasts on Thursday and Mr. Eden on Sunday

☆

'Their Finest Hour'—In honour of the Royal Navy, the Army, the R.A.F., the Merchant Navy, and the People of Britain

☆

'Victory Music-Hall' and 'The Stars Come Out' with star Variety artists

☆

Will Hay celebrates at St. Michael's

☆

The Kentucky Minstrels

☆

Jack Buchanan and Elsie Randolph in 'Stand Up and Sing'

☆

J. B. Priestley on 'Journey into Daylight'

☆

Celebrations from all parts of the United Kingdom

☆

Conan Doyle's 'The Adventure of the Speckled Band'

☆

Special Programmes for the Children

CELEBRATION

Two days after VE Day, this special issue of *Radio Times* fitted nine days of BBC Victory Programmes (Thursday 10 to Friday 18 May) into its 24 pages. Terry Freeman's cover illustration showed V searchlights beaming out of Broadcasting House in London.

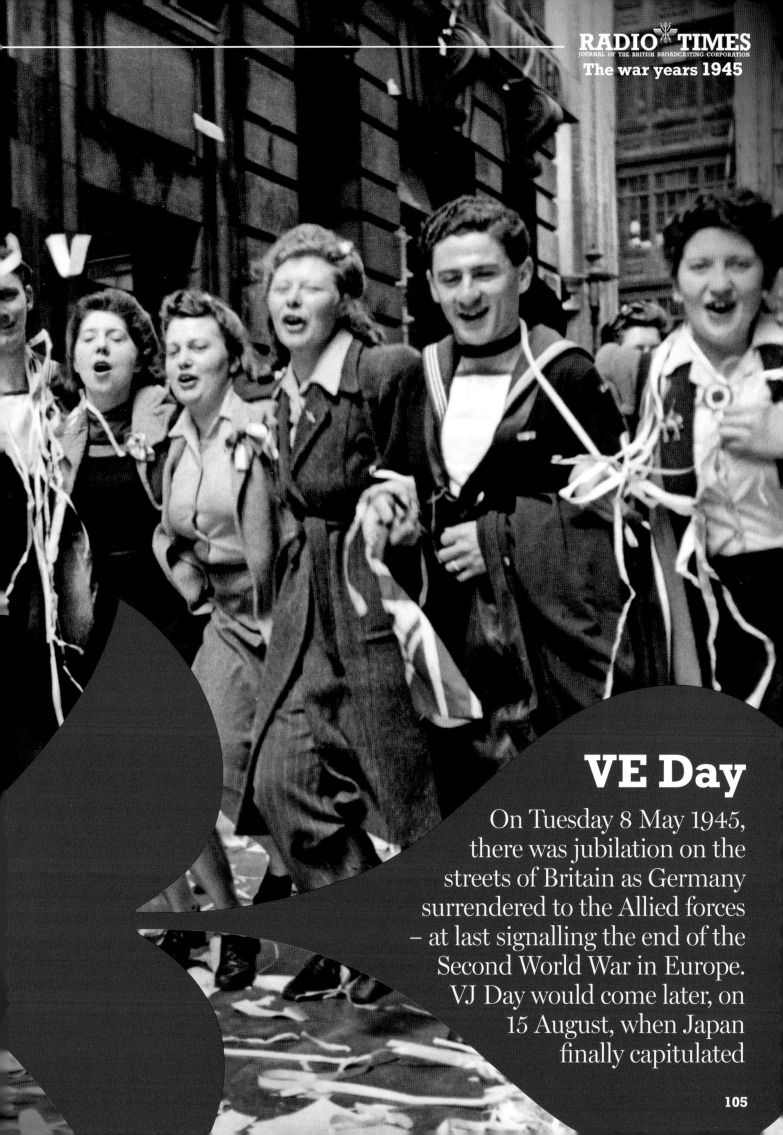

VE Day

On Tuesday 8 May 1945, there was jubilation on the streets of Britain as Germany surrendered to the Allied forces – at last signalling the end of the Second World War in Europe. VJ Day would come later, on 15 August, when Japan finally capitulated

'Indeed it is a Great Deliverance'

The ARCHBISHOP OF CANTERBURY
writes on the meaning
of our victory in Europe

To build a world worthy of our faith and sacrifice

DELIVERANCE
Geoffrey Fisher, the newly appointed Archbishop of Canterbury, wrote for *Radio Times* in May 1945 about the meaning of victory in Europe.

OPPOSITE PAGE "Their Finest Hour", the phrase from Churchill's speech of 1940, had gained currency and was used as the title of a radio dedication.

TWO questions have been put to me. What does our victory mean? How are we to celebrate it? To the first question no adequate answer can be given in a brief article; but something must be said since the meaning of our victory cannot but have its influence upon our manner of celebrating it. We discover its meaning partly by looking backwards to see what we have been delivered *from*. From rockets and flying bombs, from battles and destruction and sudden death, from the giving of life and limb in conflict, from anxiety for those on service. These things have gone from Europe, and there is a great quiet, a great relief. But it is more than that. This country has been within sight of losing its freedom, its own way of life, its existence; Europe has been within an ace of losing for centuries to come all its civilising principles; a tyranny, satanic in its methods and its ends, came near to enslaving the bodies and the minds of men. Let us not forget how near to that fatal and final disaster we were. We were on the brink of the precipice; our feet were almost gone. We kept our heads and our faith; slowly, how slowly and at what cost, the balance turned. We won back to security; we have won through. Indeed it is a great deliverance. It means that to us. The Prime Minister has said truly that it is less a triumph than a deliverance.

But we cannot assess the meaning of our victory without looking forward. *To* what are we delivered? To a second chance given to us, and perhaps the last. We had our first in 1918 and missed it. What history will say of 1945 depends on us and the other nations; and we know it. For good or ill this victory in the West is a historic moment of supreme significance; it must mark the rebirth of a Christian civilisation or its exhaustion. Which? It will be seen in the spirit in which we take our part in feeding Europe, in restoring its social and economic life, in creating a comity of nations within it, in tackling our own re-ordering of life at home. It will depend on the spirit which is disciplined and ready for hard work, honest thought, regard for others and moral rectitude. We know there is still a war to be won in the East. We know more than that: we have defended —through destruction and death we have preserved —the possibilities of civilisation. There awaits us the creative task—to build a world worthy of our faith and sacrifice.

FOR such reasons there will, I think, be and must rightly be an element of restraint in our celebrations which was shortsightedly absent in 1918. We are less light-hearted, less carefree than then, and wiser by a bitter experience. And yet at this moment of achievement, when hope is fulfilled and all the toil and sacrifice has earned its reward, we do well to let ourselves go in a great surge of emotion, in a high thanksgiving. How shall we express it? Just because it is so profound an emotion it is difficult to express, but perhaps three hints can be given.

First, we celebrate together. We are members one of another. We have seen this thing through together. As a nation, we have lived up to the traditions of our race. It is Britain which with her allies and with all liberated peoples gives thanks. In our rejoicing there is a place for pride in one another, and a great fellowship between us such as that which united us all in the dark days. Before the war we had lost that kind of pride and fellowship; in the war it has sprung to a glorious life. It will mark our celebration, because it is good and tested and true and is to be a standby to us in the tasks ahead.

BUT we are not very good, as a people, at celebrating together. We have not kept alive, as some peoples have, a great inheritance of traditional songs and dances to be the vehicle of our common emotions and to express our feelings with effectiveness. When we are in crowds we lack form. We shall do our best; but the second thing to remember is that we must keep the essential dignities of a great people at a great moment of history. There are some who do not know how to celebrate without excess or how to let themselves go without going too far. There are others who know well enough but on such an occasion forget their knowledge. But excess of that sort spoils the thing for every one and is surely out of place. For such a cause let us sing and give praise with the best that is in us.

AND thirdly, there must be a great humility in all our rejoicings. At the heart of them is the humble recognition that 'this is the Lord's doing and it is marvellous in our eyes.' If the Lord had not been on our side, or rather we for all our unworthiness on His, what might not have happened! We did all that was in us, and yet in very truth God's Providence has brought us through. It was His cause we were defending; that is why we had utter faith in it. He has answered our faith. 'Not unto us, O Lord, not unto us, but unto Thy Name be the praise.' This nation and the great men who have led it through perils of old have ever acknowledged the overruling hand of God. Shall we do less? 'O God, we have heard with our ears and our fathers have declared unto us the noble works that thou didst in their days and in the old time before them.' And now we have seen for ourselves in this our day. Then are we at our best, then are we most truly a fellowship, then are we one with our forefathers and with those that shall come after us, then do we most truly give thanks and most perfectly express it, when we stand together in the house of the Lord and lift up our hearts to the most High God. If with humble hearts we thus give to God the honour due unto His name, all our other celebrations will be touched to truth and will be honest and wholesome and good. So receiving victory at His hands, we shall give thanks and be strengthened to use it to His glory and to the true service of mankind.

A Service of Thanksgiving to Almighty God
attended by Their Majesties the King and Queen and Ministers of State will be broadcast from St. Paul's Cathedral on Sunday at 2.45 p.m.

Their Finest Hour

A series of programmes dedicated to those who have made possible this great victory in the West

THE ROYAL NAVY

Friday, 9.30 p.m.: G.F.P. on Saturday, 3.15 p.m.

TO an island nation like ours, with a maritime Empire, the Navy must always be of the first importance. Though the fundamental purpose of sea power never changes, the years have called for great changes in our Navy. Less than a hundred years ago it had to place its faith in steam, after nearly a thousand years of sail. In the last war it had, for the first time, to grope for control beneath the surface. In this war it has had to reach into the air. These transformations, always sudden in comparison with the Navy's long history, have been accomplished. This great Service has once again been equal to its task. Throughout the war it has kept the sea-routes of the world open for our use, and it has denied them to the enemy. It is right, in this hour of victory in the West, that the whole Empire should pause and salute the Royal Navy, on whose vigilance, in the last resort, depends our existence as a nation.

Now that the time has come to look back over the European War, it is perhaps fitting that Commander (now Captain) Anthony Kimmins, whose broadcasts on naval matters have pictured for us so vividly the Service to which he belongs, should be the man to tell us of the Navy's work.

He will not give us a mere diary of the sequence of naval events; nor a list of the great naval leaders whom the war has brought forth. He will tell us, rather, of the backbone of the Navy—the Bluejacket whose tradition endures while great actions are fought.

He will tell us, not so much of the famous naval engagements, as of long days and nights of monotonous routine; of endurance in Arctic or tropical waters; and of little human incidents that stand out in his mind—the flashing grin on an oil-blacked face in a ship torpedoed off Malta; how we all felt when *Exeter*, *Ajax*, and *Achilles* sent the *Graf Spee* limping to cover in Montevideo harbour; of a trip during the Battle of the Atlantic in a reserve destroyer, long overdue for the scrap-heap; and of the little ships at Dunkirk.

SOLDIERS OF BRITAIN

Monday, 9.20 p.m.: G.F.P. on Tuesday, 3.15 p.m.

IN this programme fighting men, their commanders, and war correspondents combine to tell the story of the part played by the British Army in the achievement of victory in the West. The story leads from the parade grounds of 1939 to the beaches of Dunkirk in 1940, to Commando raids from Bardia to Dieppe, through the campaigns in East and North Africa, the invasion of Sicily and then of Italy, and at last to the Normandy beaches in 1944. It recounts the hard slogging struggle for a foothold, the sweep across France, Belgium, Holland, the check at Arnhem and the Rhine; and finally the drive into the heart of the German Reich.

It is the story of the transformation of our Army from a few hundred thousand regular soldiers and territorials to a war-hardened, battle-trained citizen army of millions. It is the story of mechanised yeomanry, 'Jock' columns, of mountain troops, airborne troops, commandos, sappers, anti-tank gunners, but above all of the man who is the backbone of all armies, the infantry soldier—no longer a foot-slogging rifleman but a specialist in all the complicated techniques of war.

It is the story of armies and of commanders whose names will live in British history—of the 'thirty thousand,' the Eighth, the First, the Second; and of their leaders, Wavell, Alexander, Montgomery, Anderson, Dempsey, and the rest.

THE ROYAL AIR FORCE

Tuesday, 9.20 p.m.: G.F.P. on Wednesday, 3.15 p.m.

AN R.A.F. pilot was standing by at Manston when the call came to protect a convoy off the Isle of Wight. He took off with his squadron and saw the German planes diving over the convoy. Slipping through the clouds the British airmen got on the tail of the raiders. A burst of machine-gun fire—and the first of them had crashed to the sea in flames. The date was August 8, 1940. The Battle of Britain had begun. Only a few weeks before, the R.A.F. had been battling in the skies over France while the B.E.F. struggled back to the beaches, but the Battle of Britain was their first and probably their most brilliant effort against a ruthless and, on paper, immensely superior force.

Other battles followed, less spectacular perhaps, but again calling for almost superhuman qualities of courage and endurance.

But looking back on the R.A.F.'s achievements it isn't the weight of bombs we remember nor a campaign nor a battle, it is the men themselves. It is a Service composed of individuals, and each man has contributed his own qualities to the total effort. But because theirs is the hazard as well as the glory, it is the airmen that we remember. Flyers such as the late Paddy Finucane, who said the job he wanted after the war was something to do with figures; of MacLachlan, the one-armed intruder pilot; of Bader, the legless pilot whose example stirred so many; of Guy Gibson, the dam-buster, who went down in a later raid; of Percy ('F for Freddie') Pickard who led the brilliant Mosquito raid on the prison at Amiens; of Berry who shot down sixty flying bombs before he was posted 'missing, believed killed.'

These are only a handful of the many we know by name and of the countless others whose stories will live only in the memory of their friends and family. Because of their efforts we can go on—into victory and peace. This programme honours the memory of such men.

THE MERCHANT NAVY

Wednesday, 9.20 p.m.: G.F.P. on Thursday, 3.15 p.m.

THIS is the wartime story of an endless journey travelled by an outstandingly courageous body of fighting civilians—the merchant seamen.

In every sea, in tropic heat and in the Northern ice, in gale and calm they have sailed their ships. Old ships, new ships, rusty or freshly painted, have carried the munitions of war and our food to the places needing them.

They have undertaken their usual peacetime task, with the danger of war added to the danger of the sea. There was no need of call-up or mobilisation. We listen to their gossip and fight again with them their past battles. Jock has been in the Malta convoys, Ginger on the East Coast run, Chippie on the Russian route, 'Bose' has battled with shifting cargoes in North Atlantic gales, and we listen and remember that when Japan is defeated they have still another enemy—the sea.

These men do not blow trumpets, nor do they talk to the outside world about their exploits. But, when they meet in the world's ports, in a pub in London Docks or at a club in Montreal, they talk among themselves. They talk, too, at sea, where no landsmen can overhear them.

In this programme you will hear eight seamen telling of their adventures. There will be no fanfares of music before they speak, for their stories are not unusual nor outstanding. Men in Glasgow or Madras, Sydney, Suez or Galveston would tell you much the same tales out of the magnitude of their experiences. But they are the stories of great men.

THE PEOPLE OF BRITAIN

Thursday, 9.20 p.m.

'THE whole-hearted concurrence of scores and millions of men and women whose co-operation is indispensable, and whose comradeship and brotherhood are indispensable, is the only foundation upon which the trials and tribulations of modern war can be endured and surmounted.'

Mr. Winston Churchill spoke those words in the House of Commons on the first day of the war. *The People of Britain* is a tribute to those 'scores and millions' who, year after year, have maintained the greatest combined effort ever achieved by a nation of under forty-seven millions. It is the story of each one of us, and the common sacrifices and hardships which all have shared: munition workers, housewives, land workers, shipbuilders, members of the great civilian army which marched shoulder to shoulder with the fighting men.

We are a nation of forty-six and three-quarter million people, men and women. Of those, nine millions are children under fourteen, and another five and three-quarter millions are men over sixty-four and women over fifty-nine. This was our war potential; these were the hands and hearts and brains which manned our fighting Services, made their arms and equipment and ran the machinery of civil life in conditions of unprecedented difficulty and hardship. The official story of their efforts is contained in the statistics, tables, and graphs of the Government White Paper on the War Effort of the United Kingdom. *The People of Britain* sets out to show what this effort has meant in terms of human courage, suffering, and endurance.

'**The Battle of Britain** was their first and probably most brilliant effort against a ruthless and, on paper, immensely superior force'

'Their Finest Hour'

The Royal Air Force

Listen at 9.20 p.m. (G.F.P. 3.15 p.m. Thursday)

THEIR FINEST HOUR

As part of the BBC's celebrations, the Home Service and General Forces Programme broadcast "a series of programmes dedicated to those who have made possible this great victory in the West". They were marked in *Radio Times* by a set of illustrations by Terry Freeman.

'Their Finest Hour'

Soldiers of Britain

Listen at 9.20 p.m. (G.F.P. 3.15 p.m. Tuesda

'A war-hardened, battle-trained **citizen army of millions**'

'Their Finest Hour'

The People of Britain

Listen at 9.20 Tonight

"In this hour of victory in the West, the whole Empire should pause and salute the Royal Navy, on whose vigilance **depends our existence as a nation**"

The Royal Navy

Listen at 9.30 p.m. (G.F.P. 3.15 Saturday)

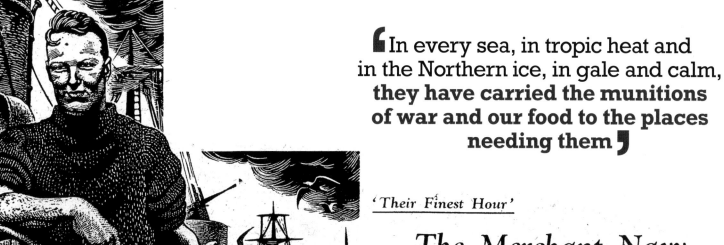

"In every sea, in tropic heat and in the Northern ice, in gale and calm, **they have carried the munitions of war and our food to the places needing them**"

'Their Finest Hour'

The Merchant Navy

Listen at 9.20 p.m.

1946

Trainload

of the Variety Department
nnected with its programm
LOFTUS WIGRAM, who
be heard on Monday even

TONIGHT AT 9.0

DARTS

Jim Pike
(News of the World)
versus
Joe Hitchcock
(St. Dunstan Four)

in 'The Match of the Year'

eight h

angle,

t-stand

VICTORY DAY PARADE

Saturday 8 June 1946 saw the official victory celebration after the
Second World War as a four-mile procession, comprising 20,000 troops
and 18 marching bands, took to the streets of London, while in the sky
there was a fly-past by 34 squadrons. Suspended since 1 September
1939, the BBC Television service resumed, with Richard Dimbleby
stationed in the Mall, adding "his word-pictures to the televised
impression of the march-past". The Radio Times cover for 2–8 June
showed a view down Whitehall, illustrated by Harold S Williamson.